# Numerology

A Beginner's Guide to Science of Numerology, Zodiac Signs and Astrology That Guides You Through the Horoscope

(The Complete Numerology Guide for Happiness and Success)

**David Javane**

Published by Rob Miles

© **David Javane**

All Rights Reserved

*Numerology: A Beginner's Guide to Science of Numerology, Zodiac Signs and Astrology That Guides You Through the Horoscope (The Complete Numerology Guide for Happiness and Success)*

ISBN 978-1-989990-38-4

All rights reserved. No part of this guide may be reproduced in any form without permission in writing from the publisher except in the case of brief quotations embodied in critical articles or reviews.

Legal & Disclaimer

The information contained in this book is not designed to replace or take the place of any form of medicine or professional medical advice. The information in this book has been provided for educational and entertainment purposes only.

The information contained in this book has been compiled from sources deemed reliable, and it is accurate to the best of the Author's knowledge; however, the Author cannot guarantee its accuracy and validity and cannot be held liable for any errors or omissions. Changes are periodically made to this book. You must consult your doctor or get professional medical advice before using any of the suggested remedies, techniques, or information in this book.

Upon using the information contained in this book, you agree to hold harmless the Author from and against any damages, costs, and expenses, including any legal fees potentially resulting from the application of any of the information provided by this guide. This disclaimer applies to any damages or injury caused by the use and application, whether directly or indirectly, of any advice or information presented, whether for breach of contract, tort, negligence, personal injury, criminal intent, or under any other cause of action.

You agree to accept all risks of using the information presented inside this book. You need to consult a professional medical practitioner in order to ensure you are both able and healthy enough to participate in this program.

# Table of Contents

INTRODUCTION ................................................................. 1

CHAPTER 1: FIVE CORE NUMBERS ................................... 4

CHAPTER 2: MOON (NUMBER – 2) ................................. 12

CHAPTER 3: PHILOSOPHY OF THE FUTURE ...................... 20

CHAPTER 4: KNOW YOUR BIRTH NUMBER AND LUCK NUMBER ........................................................................... 24

CHAPTER 5: UNDERSTANDING THE SCIENCE BEHIND NUMEROLOGY ................................................................ 28

CHAPTER 6: ORIGIN OF NUMEROLOGY ......................... 33

CHAPTER 7: YOUR MOST IMPORTANT NUMBER ............ 49

CHAPTER 8: BENEFITS OF NUMEROLOGY ...................... 56

CHAPTER 9: NUMBER ONE – THE NUMBER ONE IS ASSOCIATED WITH BEGINNINGS AND BIRTH. .................. 61

CHAPTER 10: UNDERSTANDING NUMEROLOGY ............ 77

CHAPTER 11: THE BEGINNING ........................................ 82

CHAPTER 12: WHAT IS NUMEROLOGY? ......................... 95

CHAPTER 13: WHAT, REALLY, IS NUMEROLOGY? ........... 100

**CHAPTER 14: ADVISOR AND TEACHER/CREATOR** .......... 106

**CHAPTER 15: COMBINING THE CORE ELEMENTS** .......... 120

**CHAPTER 16: YOUR ASTROLOGY** ..................................... 131

**CHAPTER 17: THE POWER OF THE BIRTHDAY** ................ 150

**CHAPTER 18: HOW TO EXPLAIN NUMEROLOGY** ............ 170

**CHAPTER 19: IF YOU BORN ON THE 9. (NINTH) OR 18TH (EIGHTEENTH), OR 27TH (TWENTY SEVEN) OF ANY MONTH THAN KINDLY READ THE FOLLOWING:** .......................... 178

**CONCLUSION** .............................................................. 182

## Introduction

It is assumed that numbers were first used before words. Current scientists and archeologists learning the ancient written world have found evidence in the form of notches carved on wood and stones and primitive abacus forms (a system used for counting) to support this theory. Numbers are teaching people about life at all times.

Numbers are embodiments of reality to a numerologist who can expand the mind and provide metaphysical, emotional, and science perspectives into life. Numbers can be perceived as waves or forces that continually change and adapt to the universe they reflect.

You can discover the power of numbers from issues that plague the heart, work, or other areas of daily life. Likewise, through art, music, science, and literature, you can see the world at large. You can develop your intuition by applying your logical mind and inner wisdom to interpret numbers. Numerology will help you understand the rewards of your life journey and encourage you to solve the internal mysteries.

There is an inherent pulse in everything in the world—and numbers are no special. In reality, every number (and letter) has its own special rhythm that has an influence on your life story. Numerology is, therefore, the study of the connection that numbers and letters have with our incidents and identity and life. It is an ancient philosophical theory that shows the outline of the future of every human being and is one of today's most detailed and effective self-help devices.

You have a soul within your physical body from a spiritual perspective that has chosen to incarnate into this life simply to evolve through the life experiences it meets while it is here. There are specific areas of development throughout this life that your soul has wanted to learn and different resources that it would like to take advantage of on its path. To do this, it requires specific personality traits and life circumstances to achieve its goal—the specifics of which can be contained in your "numbers." In other terms, the numerology profile uncovers the outline of what the spirit has pre-selected to do in this lifespan.

One of the benefits of numerology is that it can reveal the meaning of your destiny and existence and the life lessons which you experience along the way, which is valuable information if you want to make the most of your path. Numerology is more than predicting the future or selecting the ideal partner, date, or name. It's the link between who you are and who you can be. It's a step-stone that allows you to live the best of your life and be the person you can be.

## Chapter 1: Five Core Numbers

**i)PSYCHIC NUMBER:** The date you are born on is called Psychic number in Numerology.

Example - 1: If you are born on 3.9.1997, your psychic number is 3

Example – 2 If you are born on 23.10.1969, your psychic number is 2+3=5

The day you enter in to this world is not determine by you, even if you have/had an cesarean operation. You can attribute it to God OR Cosmic OR Natural forces OR Even the timely intervention of a surgeon's surgical knife. Whatever your stance. It is clear your date of birth cannot be altered. Using the Pythagorean table you can know the inherent power your birth date gives you. With that you can know what kind of likes, dislikes and character you will have (this can be applied to others as well).

In example 1: since the person born on 3.9.1997, his/her Psychic number is 3 and he/she will have the influence of number 3 from birth till the age of 18 to 22 years of age. This can be extrapolated for the 2$^{nd}$ example also.

The influence of the Psychic numbers for a person in is from birth to the age of 18-22. In this formative years the Psychic number quintessentially form the base teaching the qualities along with its challenges.

So if you know a child's Psychic number, you can know how he/she will grow up in to and what kind of quirks of character he/she will have. It can help you in terms of educating the child and also in teaching or introducing other activities suitable to his/her temperament (Music, Soccer, Chess etc.), because you know the potential of that what particular child holds. If you have a child with the Psychic number 5, you will have a hard time teaching music etc, because the concentration will be lacking in that child. If you have a child with the Psychic number 8, he/she will tend to do well in mathematics. So understanding the influence of the Psychic number, can help to enable a child to progress in his/her optimum capacity.

The detailed influences of Psychic numbers a similar to Life Path numbers, which are discussed in chapter 3. The influences are similar, the only difference is the time frame.

**ii) LIFE PATH NUMBER:** The total sum of the date (Psychic Number), month and the year you are born in

Example – 1: If you are born on 3.9.1997, your life path number is 3+9+1+9+9+7=32 and which can be reduced to 3+2=5

Example – 2: if you are born on 3.9.1969, your life path number is 3+9+1+9+6+9=37, which can be reduced to 3+7=10

The influence of Life Path numbers, supersede the influences of Psychic number when a person is around 18-22 years of age, till death. The detailed character influences of these numbers are expounded succinctly in chapter 3. Once this Life Path number takes over, it is like a guiding light house in a person's life and this is the most important number in so far as carrier, matrimony and lifelong decisions are concern for an individual. Understanding Life Path of a person is crucial in knowing the compatibility, of others like a colleagues, friends and even your life long spouse, which can help you in your social, business spheres. At the same time it can also for tell whether a partnership is going to be malignant OR benign.

**iii) KARMIC NUMBER**: Your complete name given to you at birth is your Karmic Number.(Your Name Tells About Your Character, Your Secret Desire And How You Are Seen By Others)

The 1st vowel in your name speaks volumes about your character

**FIRST VOWEL IN YOUR NAME**: It is absolutely amazing that you can floor someone whom you have just met by knowing their distinct character, just by knowing the 1<sup>st</sup> vowel of the name and with that you can tell his/her character.

Vowels are a, e, i, o, u, but in numerology the vowels are a, e. i/y, o, u. the letter "Y" is also added to this list as "Y" when uttered sounds like "I". An example of this is BYRONE, so the 1<sup>st</sup> vowel is able to give us the character of the person in accordance to the vibrations of each vowel.

Note: Read also LIFE PATH – 1 To LIFE PATH – 9 to know depth of the various characteristics of each number

Using the previous example BYRONE, since the 1<sup>st</sup> vowel is "Y" (I), which has the power of 9. So his 1<sup>st</sup> vowel will tell you his character (See Life Path 9 in Chapter 3).

**Example – 2:** If you meet a person Manoj Kishan, the 1<sup>st</sup> vowel is "A", he will possess the characteristics of Life Path 1 (See Life Path 1 in chapter 3)

From your Karmic name you get your karmic number, by adding ALL the vowels and consonants and their total sum is your Karmic Number.

For example, if your name is Tanya Nair, by using the Pythagorean table, the total sum of this name will give us 46, which can be further reduce to 4+6=10, which can be ultimately reduced to 1+0=1. So the Karmic number for this name is 1. You need to know your Karmic number, as it is one of the five core numbers. Unlike Psychic and Life Path numbers. Karmic number is with you when the name is given to you till death OR when a new name correction is done.

**4) SECTRET HEART DESIRE NUMBER:** You get this by adding all your vowels in your name (Karmic number)

**Example – 1 (BYRONE):** in this name there are 3 vowels y, o and e, so "Y" is 9, "O" is 6 and "E" is 5 and when you add all these numbers you will get 20 (9+6+5=20), which can reduce 2 (2+0=2), Since BYRONE LP 2. He is a very caring person, who can cooperate with anybody.

Example – 2: For Manoj Kishan, the vowels are "A" is 1, "O" is 6 and "I" is 9, "A" is 1, when you add all these numbers, you get 17, which can be reduced to 8.

Your name is for life, unless you choose to change it. The likelihood of a person not having any vowels in his/her name is very rare. In reality, what happens is people abbreviate their names for easy calling or because their name is too long. But as long as your given name is not changed you still have to use the vowels in your complete given name or the name you are commonly known as to people or your nickname is crucial in this respect to calibrate your secret heart desire number.

The aggregate of the vowels in your name is an indicator as to how you see yourself as. The analytics and talents you believe you possess and the desires you want to fulfil. At the same time the vowels also can tell you how your friend/colleague sees himself/herself.

**5. OUTER CHARACTER NUMBER:** you get this by adding all the consonants in your name (Karmic Number). The outer character number is what people see you as.

**Example – 1:** BYRONE, in this name "B" is 2, "R" is 9 and "N" is 5, by adding all these numbers will get 16, which can reduced to 1+6=7 (See Life Path 7 in chapter 3), BYRONE will be seen as a stoic introvert deep in thought living in his own world with little social skills.

Example – 2: In Manoj Kishan's case, the letters "M" is 4, "N" is 5, "J" is 1, "K" is 2, "S" is 1, "H" is 8 and "N" is 5 are the consonants. When add them up, we get 26, which can reduced to 2+6=8 (see Life Path 8). He will be seen by others as a person seeking money and worldly goals.

## Chapter 2: Moon (Number – 2)

People who are born under the dates 2, 11, 20 or 29 or the date total by adding all the digits of the date to single number which becomes 2 or as per numerology if the name total gives sum 2 are coming under MOON power.

Number 2 indicates Moon and it gives life to the entire people mind. Either the date is giving total of 2 or as per numerology if the name gives number 2 (means 2, 11, 20 or 29), these people are famous and earn bad name also in everything. They must have strong belief in life or job or self confidence and that will help them to do wonders in life.

Otherwise life will be useless by gaining cursing from others.

They are able to advise others to improve in life and to be on top. But coming to the own life many times they think more number of times before executing anything by wasting time and energy.

Unwanted fear must be removed from mind and should improve will power, self confidence and courage. Then only life will be in a good shape. People under 2 must improve in affirmative thinking and good imagination of the positive side to avoid disasters in life.

People born under 2 may have good relationship with 1,3,4,7 and sometimes 8 born ones.

No addiction to be on anything for these people as addictive things like coffee, tea, alcohol etc may spoil entire life. Sometimes they are affected by diabetes and eye problems.

**People born under 2:** May have good imagination with high level of thoughts. Fear and calmness are some qualities of 2 born people. Good will power and research minded. Many are famous writers.

**People born under 11:** They believe in god and naturally having blessings. Belief is the strength and belief & confidence are the best qualities to achieve anything.

**People born under 20:** Effectively guide others and may become divine guide or guru to a group of people. But do be selfish as that may lead to disaster.

**People born under 29:** May fight with others always and being with own benefits sometimes disturb others too much. As many bad qualities occupy these people naturally; they have to be monitored by parents from childhood and good things to be taught.

Names and Number 2:

You will be ruled by MOON or the number 2 if you have the name total as 1 by adding up all the alphabets numbers making a single digit. (Example: ILAYA RAJ = 1+3+1+1+1+2+1+1 =

But, remember that the people born under 2 and 7 (either the date or sum of date digits) only can have names under 2. Then only it will give good results. For others it may give trouble and lot of failures in life mostly. Mostly avoid names under 2.

So, check the numbers and alphabets in the introduction chapter and find your name digits or sum accordingly. If not lucky, change letters or names to good numbers as said above.

**Good and Bad Numbers Under 2 (for names by adding all the alphabets' digits)**
**2** – Single letter name is not considered like B, K, R etc.. So let us ignore this 2 for name.

Also if any name comes under 2 then consider the previous prediction given above.

**11** – By believing god, they go up in life. Easily these people earn profit with the same belief.

Unexpected situation and dangers may arise sometimes and proper caution required always.

**20** – If these people are selfish and try for bigger things, then they may lose everything finally. If helping nature to others are cultivated, entire world may follow them and appreciate.

**29** – Not so good for family life. Other people may laugh at life. May appear in front of judge many times or cases/argument happen quite often. Most of the people will have temporary friendship with others.

**38** – Straight forward people and calm. Few times may have kingdom like status and live high level of life. Also many people may trouble and may throw out without any breathing time. Sudden downfalls and life may end up with tragedy.

**47** – Good improvement in life. Earn money quickly under any business or work. Very lucky people & sometimes may have eye problems. If these people want to lead good life; they must be pure vegetarian. Should not kill animals or any living things.

**56** – Excellent number to get divine powers. Prosperity, abundance, health and wealth altogether success in life. Some people are magicians. Should be very careful during middle or aged times as there may be a chance to lose everything.

**65** – Very good number to have divine powers and blessings. Others will help very much.

Good for family life and sometimes there will be minor troubles physically and in career too!

**74** – Good for social lead and related life. May not become rich and always there will be incomplete tasks pending.

**83** – May win everything. Life picks up with uptrend always. Luxurious life is the boon for these people naturally. Higher status and designation too!

**92** – 100% excellent number for Prosperity, abundance, health, wealth & winning. They may attain siddhi powers easily. Lots of secrets will be revealed by divine.

**101** – Not so good number under Moon.

**Lucky Days:** 7, 16 & 25 are good. (Either day or sum of the digits in date).25 is powerful.

Days under 1 also will help.

**Important Days:** 2, 11, 20 and 29. But good luck will work out automatically. Don't start any new task these days.

**Unlucky Days:** 8, 9, 18, 26 and 27. Avoid all the good start-ups or do not start anything in life in these days.

**Work/Business:** Most of the work/Business will be helpful for people under 2 if they work hard. Also agriculture, textiles, milk plant, coffee/tea, fancy items, jewellery, liquid items, beauty and cosmetics, medicines, paints, photo/ films studio, writing, divine products, religious, food items business areas are best.

**Marriage/ Life Partner:** People under 2 may choose 7 people as their life partners mainly. 3, 4 and 6 people are also good for them.

**Lucky Colours:** Green, Yellow and White.

Lucky Metal: **Silver.**

**Lucky Stone:** Jade and Moon Stone.

Personalities Under Number 2:

M.K GANDHI – 02-10-1869 (2 & 9)

THOMAS ALVA EDISON – 11-02-1771 (2 & 6)

C. SUBRAMANYA BHARATHI – 11-12-1882 (2 & 6)

ADOLF HITLER – 20 – 04 – 1889 (2 & 5)

## Chapter 3: Philosophy Of The Future

In all the larger shaping of a life, there is a plan already, into which one has no choice but to fit. Helen Keller said, "Many people know so little of what is beyond their short range of experience. They look within themselves and find nothing. Therefore, they conclude that there is nothing outside themselves either." Bertrand Russell wrote: "Unless man increases his wisdom as much as his knowledge, increase of knowledge will only be increase of sorrow." In the Gita, Krishna says, "It is the knowledge of matter with its evolution and the spirit, which are considered as wisdom." This means that if we want to understand the total reality and meaning of our lives, we need to understand two universal concepts that influence us — science and spirituality.

Our quest for knowledge is called science. The word is derived from the Latin $^{scio}$, which means $^{I\ know}$. In the Indian context, we have the word Veda, derived from the Sanskrit word, $^{vid}$, also meaning $^{to\ know}$. But this is where the similarities end. Science is limited to the outer physical world of objects, but as is known, material well-being alone cannot lead to total fulfilment.

Whereas, Veda (or Vedanta) deals with the knowledge of both the outer (physical) and inner (psycho-spiritual) worlds.

For modern science, the centre of gravity is outside of man himself, where he is simply treated as an object. Though science has wiped out many of man's fears and uncertainties, it has also helped create in him new fears and apprehensions. As Einstein concluded "Science can denature plutonium, but it cannot denature evil in the heart of man."

On the contrary, the Vedas testify that the Indian sages of yore were great spiritual scientists. They felt that science minus spirituality will have a deleterious effect on humankind. There is no totality of human experience in science as it includes only a part of human experience.

On the other hand, spirituality is a science of values — the pivotal point on which depends the progress and survival of mankind. Arthur Koestler said, "Physics turns into metaphysics with a flavour of mysticism." This is true of Vedic seers who were spiritualists and scientists par excellence as they knew

what to reveal for universal application or restrict to a few worthy minds and hands. Universal well-being calls for integration of the above two energy streams.

Unfortunately, during our progressive years, all our efforts are directed, coaxed, focused and channelized towards gaining credits. Very little opportunity is given to understand the importance of a vision and the essential philosophy behind it. During many innings of servitude, the one quality ingrained in us is the art of airing our uncalled-for and unwarranted views with no logic or sagacity. Unless this inadvertent provocation is eradicated, we will be devoid of developing a vision in our life.

From birth, we have been using all the five senses. But even after progressing academically, we fail to inculcate an urgency to use that one aspect which has marked this progress — sensibility. Probably, the five senses veto the architect of our future, the sixth sense. Hence, it should be our earnest endeavour in every situation to develop a philosophical bent of mind. Academic excellence alone does not guarantee success in life. The emotional quotient should be appropriately mixed. Because ultimately, success in one's life depends upon IQ + EQ + SQ, namely, Intelligence Quotient + Emotional Quotient + Spiritual Quotient.

## Chapter 4: Know Your Birth Number And Luck Number

The Whole Universe is governed by Planetary Numbers One to Nine. Each and every human being landed on the stage of world is assigned a number in accordance with his /her date of birth which is categorized according to Planetary Number under which he/she is born

1,10 ,19, 28 of any month is assigned Birth number and is associated with Planet Sun, whose Number is One.

2,11,20, 29 of any month is assigned birth number 2 and is associated with Moon, whose Number is Two

3, 12, 21, 30 of any month is assigned birth number 3 and is associated with Jupiter, whose Number is three.

4,13, 22, 31 of any month is assigned birth number 4 is associated with Uranus, whose number is four.

5, 14, 23 of any month is assigned birth number 5 and is associated with Mercury, whose number is five

6, 15, 24 of any month is assigned birth number 6 and is associated with Venus, whose number is six

7, 16, 25 of any month is assigned birth number 7 and is associated with Neptune, whose number is seven

8, 17, 26 of any month is assigned birth number 8 and is associated with Saturn, whose number is eight

9, 18, 27 of any month is assigned birth number 9 and is associated with Mars, whose number is nine

Hence, a person who is categorized under a particular Planetary Number will develop qualities related to that planet and his life will be influenced by it. Friendly and unfriendly numbers of the particular planet will interact throughout his life, shaping his life accordingly.

Personal attainments are governed by Birth number and luck is governed by your luck number

For knowing your luck number, count sum total of your birth date, month and year. For example 2.7.1981 2+7+1981- 2+7+1+9+8+1= 28 = 2+8=10=1+0=1. Hence your birth no. is 2 and luck no. is 1 and so what is in store for you due to your personal efforts, read predictions for no. 2 and what is in store for you due to luck, read predictions for number 1

Knowledge of Numerology helps to know our strengths and weaknesses, helps in accomplishment of our destiny by creating a positive environment and wiping out negative energy. It paves way to excellence in professional and personal life n helps us to know and shape our future.

In Numerology, Numbers are manipulated to pave the path of life smoother for you. Numerology can provide guidance for any aspect of life i.e. education, health issues, personality grooming, career orientation, job, change in job profile and business, business expansion, matrimonial alliance, raising family, adoption, love marriage, divorce, business deals, partnership, investment tips, political career, property dealing, naming ceremony, naming your firm and residence, domesticity and adjustment in all walks of life. It guides and helps us to lead a better life.

## Chapter 5: Understanding The Science Behind Numerology

In the book 'The Secret Doctrine', Helen P. Blavatsky has written that there were secret laws that were always passed orally from the teachers to the students for thousands of years! It was ensured that they would never write down the teachings since they never wanted people with profane minds to use these theories wrongly or incorrectly. This is because of the fact that they may use these theories to obtain what they want the most. She had also stated that these theories would be revealed to people who are honestly looking to seek what they needed to. These people would find that the ideas would be revealed to them only when they are ready. This information would only be used to enlighten the minds of the people of the day since there is no other person out here who would be able to understand how you may have felt.

There are certain authors who have been trusted with the knowledge and to part with it as well. There will be a lot more people in the future who will be able to help in the propagation of the knowledge. This is true since I would not have been able to provide you with this knowledge if it had not been spread in this age. Why do you think I have been able to gather all this information? And why do you think I am imparting it to you now? It is because of the fact that you and I are keen to learn more about ourselves. As children of this age, we will not stop asking questions since we do not know what the ancient man had experienced when he had seen the world form. He would have been a lucky man since there were no opinions that would have formed at the time. The ancient man would never have had to go too far to experience the beauty since they were very close to the forests where they could listen to the sound of the birds and experience the beauty and stillness of nature.

The above had only happened right before men could parrot the opinions of other men. This was when they had always learnt what they needed to know by meditating and understanding themselves better. This is because of the fact that they would be able to join with their Higher Selves to attain the greater consciousness of the Universe around them. You have to remember that you are the divine substance of God and you are the one who possesses the intelligence of your creator!

You may have read numerous books that are related to what numerology is and may have also learned more about the different techniques. There could only be some that may have struck a chord with you. You will be able to find yourself only through the process of meditation, reasoning and insights. It is when you do this that you will be able to fit all the pieces of the puzzle together. The secret to your life has always been hidden in a place that seems very obvious. The science behind numerology lies in the realm of transcendental physics, which has entwined with the geometry and the symbolism of the different numbers. There are certain truths that have been hidden in magic, math and myths. There are some sources that have stated that the mysteries would never be revealed. They would take a key idea and then surround it with different material, which would help in tarnishing the idea in general. If you were someone who is truly seeking the knowledge, you would definitely gather the idea that has been stated in the books.

It is true that most of the ideas were based on the letters in Hebrew, including their numbers and it has been understood that neither could be interchanged. The meaning behind your life could be understood with the shapes and the letters that have always been considered the manifestation of your virtues. These represent the power of a determinable and a set nature, which would be revealed to a person when they meditate to understand their life better. You will find it easier if you meditate on a particular symbol if you are trying to make it reveal itself to you. It is best to understand these symbols since they are the universal language spoken by your soul. It is because of this that Pythagoras had his students meditating on different symbols and also share the meanings that they had derived through the course of the meditation. He also taught his students that numbers were living qualitative realities that would always represent the rate and the state of vibrations.

You will learn through the course of this book about how you can meditate to understand the different symbols. You will also be able to understand the different symbols that you would be using to read and understand your future.

## Chapter 6: Origin Of Numerology

No one knows of the exact time or origin of numerology, but by 500 BC, Chaldeans, Hebrews, Chinese and Indians had their own versions of this pseudo science. Several great scholars have contributed to this subject and the noteworthy among them is Pythagoras who was a Greek philosopher, mathematician, astronomer and a renowned numerologist who lived around 500 BC and is best known for one of his theorems, known as Pythagoras's theorem in mathematics. Pythagoras is known as "The father of Mathematics" and also "The father of Numerology". Pythagorean numerology is the most popular of all numerology systems. Chinese emperor Yu is said to be the father of Chinese Lo-shu grid numerology. The other noteworthy numerologist in the early nineteenth century is Chiero, who advocated the Chaldean system. And many more unsung heroes have contributed to this subject in their own style.

## TAROT NUMEROLOGY

n the following chapters, I will help you to calculate certain key numbers that influence the theme of your life. For each name number there will be a tarot card associated with it. This tarot card is just a pictorial description that will help you better understand this subject. The native can use this name numerology as a compass to seek the greater purpose and meaning in their lives and career and get some indicators to know more about what motivates and energizes them. The natives can also employ behavior change techniques to increase or decrease the frequency of behavioral patterns, such as altering an individual's response to stimuli.

There are 78 tarot name cards in all. These cards are classified into two types:

Major Arcane covers numbers from 0 - 22

Minor Arcane covers numbers 23 - 78

The Minor Arcana, is further sub classified into 4 suits namely the Wands, Pentacles, Swords and Cups to represents the four elements of nature namely Fire, Earth, Air and Water respectively.

Suit of Wands

The Suit of Wands represents the element Fire and is associated with the Aries, Leo and Sagittarius signs of the zodiac. Wands are primarily associated with the spirit of the human beings in the following forms:

Motivation

Determination

Ambition

Celebration

Competition

Victory

Progression

Empowerment

Strife & Struggle

Responsibility

Self-sacrifice

The negative aspects of the Suit of Wands include illusion, impulsiveness, lack of direction or purpose, retardation, irresponsible behavior, feeling victimized, being disorganized and leading a chaotic lifestyle. The Suit of Wands traditionally represents summer season and South East direction.

Suit of Pentacles

The Suit of Pentacles represents the element Earth that covers the more mundane aspects of life such as work, business, assets, money and other material possessions. Pentacles are connected through the senses and seek pleasurable experiences. They represent the Earth signs of Taurus, Virgo, and Capricorn. The main themes around which the natives fall under the Suit of Pentacles are:

Manifestation

Multitasking

Teamwork

Objectivism

Realization

Charity

Accumulation

Perfection

Material Security

Prosperity

The lower octaves of the Suit of Pentacles include possessiveness, financial loss, poverty, overly materialistic attitude, over-indulging, and being workaholic to the detriment of other life priorities. In addition, there may be blockages in being able to manifest ideas and plans resulting in a lack of financial success. Tangible goals and perfect planning is very essential for the recipe of success. The Suit of Pentacles traditionally represents autumn season and South West direction.

Suit of Swords

Swords represent the Air signs of Aquarius, Libra and Gemini. The Suit of Swords deals with the mind and the intellect and is primarily associated with the following actions:

Will power

Zen

Trust

Liberty

Self centeredness

Compassion

Craft

Autocracy

Apprehensions

Freedom of thought

Generally speaking an action can be both constructive and destructive and is considered to be the most powerful as well as the most dangerous of all the four suits. However, the Swords can be balanced by spirit and emotions. On the flipside, Swords can be violent, cunning, suspicious, selfish, imprisoned, confrontational, ruthless, rigid, temperamental, guilty, judgmental and insensitive. The Suit of Swords traditionally represents winter or spring season and North West direction.

Suit of Cups

The Suit of Cups corresponds to the water signs of Cancer, Scorpio and Pisces in the zodiac. Water symbolizes the subconscious mind, reason and deals primarily with the following human emotions:

Ardent Desire

Faith & Commitment

Joy of sharing

Humility

Counting thy Blessings

Parent Child Relationship

Prayer

Passion

Contentment

Family bondage

The negative aspects of the Suit of Cups include being overly emotional or completely detached, dispassionate, depressed, resentful, crying over spilled milk, egoistic attitude, manipulative, greedy and setting unrealistic expectations. Also there may be repressed emotions and an inability to truly express oneself. Cups traditionally represent autumn season and North East direction.

Make your own Numerology Chart

Now comes the interesting part. Take a paper and pen and draw a table as shown below:

My Numerology Chart

| | |
|---|---|
| 1 | Birth Number |
| 2 | Destiny Number |
| 3 | Calling Name Number |
| 4 | No. of Alphabets in Calling Name |
| 5 | Calling Name – Vowels |
| 6 | Calling Name – Consonants |
| 7 | Key Compound Number |

Know your Birth Number

Reduce your birth number to a single digit. If you are born on 14th, then reduce it to single digit by adding 1 and 4. So your birth number will be 5 and this Birth Number reveals your main talent. Update My Numerology Chart - Row number 1 with your Birth Number.

Know your Destiny Number

Destiny number complements your Birth Number with a very specific talent or strength that greatly facilitates the fulfillment of your destiny. Calculate your personal destiny number by adding the day, month and year of your birth and reduce it to a single digit.

Say your birthday is 29-4-1985.

Then you will have to add birthday+month+y + e + a+r In this case, it will be 29+4+1+9+8+5 = 56

Update My Numerology Chart - Row number 2 with your Destiny Number.

Calculate your Name Number

Come on let's calculate your name number using the following chart.

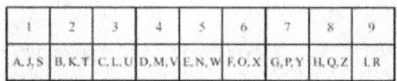

Let's now calculate your calling name number, for example say 'Charan'

C H A R A N

3 + 8 + 1 + 9 + 1 + 5 = 27

Update My Numerology Chart - Row No. 3 with the Total Name Number derived.

Count the number of Alphabets

Total Number of alphabets in "Charan" is 6. Now update "My Numerology Chart - Row No. 4 with the total number of alphabets in your name.

Calculate the Vowel Number

In English, A, E, I, O, U are considered as vowels. However, in Numerology, acknowledging a letter as either a vowel or a consonant is sometimes handled differently than it is in linguistics. For example, in the word "Mystic," the letter "Y" is a vowel. And in the word "Ramayana", the letter "y" should be considered a consonant as it comes before a vowels. Y is again considered as a consonant if the word starts with Y, for e.g. Yin Yang. Update "My Numerology Chart - Row No. 5 with the total vowel number.

In the name "Charan", there are two A's.

So the total vowel number is

A A

1 + 1 = 2

Calculate the Consonant Number

Now subtract the Total Vowel number from the Total Name Number. In the example, 27 - 2 = 25 (will be the total consonant number). Update My Numerology Chart - Row No. 6 with the total consonant number.

My interpretations for that Rider-Waite Cards with respect to your name number will be discussed in the following chapter.

Calculate the Key Compound Number

Key compound number is just the base number that is acquired by adding the complete usage name. Say the name is Edgar Cayce.

Edgar = 5 + 4 + 7 + 1 + 9 = 26 - keyl = 2 + 6 = 8

Cayce = 3 + 1 + 7 + 3 + 5 = 19 - key 2 = 1 + 9 = 10 = 1

Key Compound Number = key 1 + key 2 = 8 + 1 = 9

Now update My Numerology Chart - Row No. 7 with the key compound number.

Thumb Rules of Numbers

Just like Birth Number and Destiny Number, your Name Number provides important information about your strength, talents and weaknesses and it indicates your deepest yearnings and what motivates you most. It also provides information about the characteristics you show or hide in public and about the impression you're likely to make on others. There are also certain rules that are applicable to this name numerology that is listed below. If you come across any of these conflicts in your chart, then you are likely to face several hurdles in your life as these particular conflicts have an over-riding effect on your name number.

Natives with name numbers 1, 10, 19 and 28.... should not have 6, 15, 24....series as number of alphabets and vice versa

Natives with name numbers 3, 12, 21 and 30.... should not have 6, 15, 24....series as number of alphabets and vice versa

No name number should have 16 alphabets in total

Number Thirteen and Sixteen should not form in as compound name numbers

Those with name number 7, 16, 25, 34, 43, 52, 61 and 70 should make sure that the vowels and consonants do not form a Sun-Venus conflict

Those with name number 9, 18, 27, 36 should make sure that

the vowels and consonant do not form a Jupiter-Venus conflict

Titles like Jr., Sr., Dr., Prince, King, Pope, Sir, Madam, Queen and Princess etc., should be ignored in all calculations

Picture Illustrations

About 3000 years ago, during the Pythagoras period, the King was supposed to be treated as God. Anyone who opposed this idea was executed like Socrates. So Pythagoras came up with the idea of Tarot cards with esoteric symbols, colours and themes to explain Numerology, the divine secret of the Universal Intelligence without confronting the King and yet propagating this subject through secret schools. As the time passed, different schools of numerology emerged as each picture can be interpreted in different ways. I have come up with my own interpretation of each and every Tarot deck by studying 0.2 million famous peoples' history in the last 3.5 years.

Your Name Numbers

In this section all the name numbers starting from 0 to 78 will be discussed in detail. Well no one has a name number zero. But, I have just kept this as a tradition that has come for the last three thousand years. For every name I have given a pictorial description so that you can understand better. There are several tarot decks in the market that depict each number, and I chose to use my own deck of cards which reflects the culture of my motherland without diluting the essence of the pictures.

Also the tarot decks have traditionally followed a sequence of Wands, Cups, Swords and Pentacle suits representing one-fire, two-emotions, three-air, and four-earth respectively. However, I was not convinced with this idea. The universally accepted twelve signs of zodiac that start with Aries, then Taurus, Gemini, Cancer, Leo, Virgo, Libra, Scorpio, Sagittarius, Capricorn, Aquarius and Pisces are repeated with a sequence of fire, earth, air and water elements. I too prefer to go by this sequence. I have also quoted some examples of great personalities who have strongly influenced our world and surroundings. Please note that I have used only their usage names but not the name given at their birth while quoting their examples. If your name number is greater than 78, then you will have to read the key compound name number description only.

## Chapter 7: Your Most Important Number

This number is called your "Life Path" number in Numerology, and is by far the most important of the four main numbers. It is based on all the numbers in your date of birth. All you do is make a sum, like the illustration below, add it up and bring the final result down to a single digit.

Let's take someone born on 9 December 1946 as our example. We simply make up a sum of his day, month and year of birth and added it up. This gives us a total of 1967. Now add the 1,9,6, and 7 which gives us a total of 23. Finally we add the 2 and the 3 together which gives us a final total of 5. This persons most important number (Life Path Number) is 5.

There are two exceptions to this rule, unfortunately. These occur whenever your total comes down to an 11 or a 22. These are known as Master Numbers in Numerology and give the person with them special capabilities. Each time you arrive at either 11 or 22, stop there and do not reduce it further. Here's an example:

2

1944 = 1975

1975 and 1+9+7+5=22

My friend, born on a leap year (29th February, 1944) has a Life Path number of 22, so it does not get reduced to a 4.

Already you have all the information you need to work out the most important number relating to you, but before we go on I'll briefly explain the meanings of each number.

If your Life Path number is 1, you have to learn to stand on your own two feet and achieve a degree of independence. This may not be easy early on in life, but is essential for your progress in this life.

If 2 is your most important number, you have to learn to cooperate and fit in to group situations. You will be tactful and diplomatic, and will be happier inside a partnership, like marriage, rather than being entirely on your own.

3 is a fortunate number, as it is the number of self-expression. This means that you have to communicate in some sort of way-possibly through singing, dancing, talking or writing. With this number you will be learning all the way through life, but may sometimes lack the motivation.

With a Life Path number of 4 you will have to work hard to achieve your goals. You will be well organised and capable, but could feel hemmed in or restricted at times. 4 is the number that always gets there, but with a great deal of effort.

5 is the number of freedom and variety, so if this is your most important number, you will be versatile and capable at almost

everything you attempt. However, this versatility may make it hard to work out what it is you really want to do in this life, so you could be something of a rolling stone, and a 'jack-of-all- trades'. The big advantage of this number is that it is the number of youth, so you will always be young at heart.

With a Life Path number of 6, home and family will be extremely important to you, and your greatest happiness and satisfactions in life will come with people close to you. At times you may be responsible for more than your fair share, but you will always be positive and ready to give a helping hand.

7 is the number of wisdom and knowledge. If this is your Life Path number, you will operate on a slightly different level than most people, which may make you feel as if you are apart from others at times. However, in the long run, you will be growing and learning within,

and will ultimately build up a strong faith in life.

8 can be a stubborn, rigid number, but is an extremely fortunate number to have as a lucky one, as it is the number of money. If this is your most important number you will have definite material needs, and will be prepared to work hard to achieve them. When you have achieved your goals, you'll be generous with your money, but it might be a bit hard to separate you from your money before that time!

With a Life Path number of 9, you will be a humanitarian at heart, always wanting to help others in need. This is a very giving number, and you will get great satisfaction out of helping others. However, you must remain aware of your own needs, so do not let others take advantage of your good nature.

11 is the first of the two Master Numbers. If this is your most important number you will be good at coming up with ideas, but

you must make sure that they are practical before trying to put them into practice. This is also the number of illusion and daydreaming, so make sure that you do actually do something, rather than simply dreaming about all the great things you are going to do one day.

The final number is 22. With this as your Life Path number, you can literally achieve anything you set your mind upon. You should always aim high, as you could succeed on an international level. This number can take parts from all the other umbers and really make things happen. Unfortunately, there is always a degree of nervous tension associated with 11 and 22, which can work against these people's best interests early on in life.

Now, how can we use this number?

Use this number any time you need a single number. If you are in a lottery at work, utilize your Life Path number. Remember, also, that you can use the multiples of the number as well, as long as you can reduce them to your main number. For instance, if your Life Path number was 5, you could also use 14,23,32,41,59,68, 77, 86 and 95 as these all reduce down to 5. Naturally, you could go on almost indefinitely. 1967, as we saw earlier, reduces to a 5. With Master number you can also go backwards as well as forwards. So, with a Life Path number of 22, 4 could be used just as well as 88.

This is where things start to get a little complicated. What we are going to do now is turn all the letters in your name at birth into numbers using the following chart.

## Chapter 8: Benefits Of Numerology

Now that you have a general idea of what numerology is, you may be wondering what the benefit is for you to study numerology. While many people are casual observers of numerology, Googling their numbers and taking quizzes to find out what that number means, for the more serious practitioners, there are several benefits. The more you use numerology and open your mind to what the numbers tell you, the more you'll see these benefits making changes in your life.

Here are a few of the top benefits of using numerology:

Teaches You about Yourself

Everyone struggles a little with identity. Who are you? Why are you on this earth? While learning all the answers to these questions might take time, numerology can help make clear what influences there are in your life. By learning this, you'll better be able to understand what your character strengths and weaknesses are and how to self-improve. You'll also have a better understanding of why the same patterns keep occurring in your life and why you seem to constantly make certain decision. With prolonged use of numerology, you'll gain a true sense of identity.

## Brings Clear Understanding to Relationships

Just like numerology can bring you a better understanding of who you are, it can bring an understanding of what you need, and therefore who you need, in a relationship. By making clear to you what your expectations are in relationships and what others expect from you, you'll be able to start new relationships with clarity. And, it can help you understand the dynamics of your current relationships, both the positive and the negative. As you grow more and more aware of these things, you'll find your relationships improving and those that can't be salvaged will slowly fade away.

Helps You Realize Opportunities

Certain numbers in numerology can help you be more aware of when you're being presented with opportunities. Sometimes, with all the craziness of life, it's easy to overlook moments and chances that could lead you to bigger and better things. However, with numerology, some of the guesswork is removed. You can move forward and grab opportunities with a sense of clarity, because you know that the moments are coming and have an idea of where they'll lead.

Teaches Life Lessons

In numerology there is a number called a Karmic Debt Number. This shows how balanced you are on the karmic scale and whether you need to put more good into the world or not. By knowing your karmic number, you can adjust your life to transform into a better version of yourself.

While it may take some time to change the way you live, every little bit counts. If you stick with it, you'll find more good karma coming your way.

Encourages True Balance

When it comes down to it, the one thing everyone wants in their life is true balance. Whether this is in relationships, at work, or at home, balance is a goal everyone strives to achieve. In the end, that's what numerology is about: Clarifying the ways you can bring more balance to your life. Because you're more aware of yourself, your emotions and reactions to life will be more balanced. Your relationships will balance out and become healthier. All from the clarity that numerology brings.

While it's not a magic bullet, numerology has many benefits that it can impart to you, if you keep your mind open and are willing to make changes in your life. Many believe that following numerology can lead you to the destiny you were supposed to achieve. While it may take a little work and a little changing on your part, following numerology and studying the power of your numbers can benefit and change your life.

## Chapter 9: Number One – The Number One Is Associated With Beginnings And Birth.

It is the number of creation. The symbol of one is the dot and its planet is the sun. Anyone whose ruling number is one will instinctively be a leader. In almost any situation they will instinctively want to take charge. One's tend to have high energy levels and amazing willpower and if they set their mind on something then they will achieve it. They are naturally good at coming up with ideas but their impatience can mean that they lack the methodical ability to see things through to the finish. They can be vain for they have faith in themselves and their abilities and don't like to play second fiddle to anyone. Also their impatience can lead to outbursts of temper, especially when someone dares to stand in their way. They like to take centre stage and hold court and astrologically they are most closely linked to the sign of Leo. These people will have a great sense of drama and know how to put on a show. But any failings tend to be mediated by their great sense of humour and they tend to be kind and compassionate because one also rules the heart. Generosity will be expressed whenever possible and they would make great fund raisers for they can sweep others along with the strength of their convictions.

Because of their close links to the sun these people are born to shine. They are often drawn to arenas where they can express themselves in public, for example as entertainers of politicians. They will also have a tendency to stand aloof. A person with the ruling number of one will not need a lot of support. They will have a strong independent streak and be able to take care of themselves. What they will really want from other people is an audience. These people are not so good in a supporting role. In a crisis their instinct will always be to lead or take charge. They help people by taking practical action.

Number Two – the number two is represented by a straight line. If you put two dots on a sheet of paper and then join them, a straight line would be the result. Two is obviously the number of togetherness. Twos tend to be emphatic and feeling; they are caring sensitive feeling who can be more concerned with other people's feelings than their own. Twos are natural empaths and are often able to sense how someone else is feeling without having to speak; they make good counsellors. Two are the nurturing types; they do not usually like to lead but are happy to work in groups, especially when allowed to exercise their sympathetic skills. Two are excellent companions and devoted and loyal friends, they are usually good parents but must guard against a tendency to smother and over-protect their children. Twos are linked astrologically to the sign of Cancer and therefore to the Moon. Their moods can fluctuate like the Moon; they are generally more pessimistic than ones. Twos are usually good homemakers who often like cooking, gardening and interior design. Their houses are warm and comfortable and visitors will be well fed and looked after.

Number Three – Three is the number of exploration. All threes love to travel, not just in the physical sense but mentally as well. Three like to study and will be particularly interested in philosophy and religion. Threes can be rebellious and don't like to play by the rules but this is also part of their exploration; sometimes they like to push the rules to see how far they can go and still get away with things. The danger is they will push too far and end up in serious trouble. The symbol of three is the triangle which is one of the strongest structures, used in building pyramids. Three are not the most methodical of numbers, meaning that they have an ad hoc spontaneous approach to life. They are often attracted to alternative life styles; a nine to five job in an office would be anathema to them.

Threes tend to be free spirits with more than a touch of gypsy in their souls. They are tolerant of others and do not tend to force their views of anyone but they expect others to be tolerant of them. With their love of philosophy they can be deep thinkers and they enjoy probing the big questions of life. Three is linked to the planet Jupiter; threes are renowned for their sense of fun, they tend to be sociable and are often lucky. They have a knack for being in the right place at the right time.

Number Four – Four are the rationalists; they have a love of method and logic. Four is the number of the square. They are all very hard workers and hate to leave a job unfinished. They can be workaholics. Give them a list of tasks to do and they will be happy. They will do every task, one at a time and always do a job to the best of their ability, regardless of what it is they've been asked to do. They are not the best leaders because they can get bogged down in the details and find it hard to see the big picture but they are happy to be a small cog in a big machine. They are attracted to things like the military and the police which deal with order and control.

They can be control freaks and like to do everything exactly by the rules. The danger is that they can be inflexible and find it hard to make allowances for circumstances where the rules might actually be wrong. But they have tremendous energy and perseverance and rarely seem to get tired. Their stamina is legendary. Four is linked to the planet Saturn. Fours can have difficulty relaxing and letting their hair down. They are notoriously hard task masters but they are always hardest on themselves. Satisfying their exacting high standards is never an easy task.

Number Five – Five is the number of communication. Fives spend a lot of time speaking on the phone, texting and answering their e-mails. Their lives tend to be a gigantic social whirl and whatever job they do, you can bet that their communication skills will be a huge part of it. Fives will be good at multi-tasking for they have a reputation of being a jack-of-all-trades, the danger is that their knowledge will always be superficial and they will really know nothing in depth. They are good at starting things but not so good at finishing them. As soon as the task becomes boring they tend to abandon it for fresher pastures. They also spread themselves too thinly on occasion leaving themselves over-worked and stressed out.

The symbol of five is the five pointed star or pentagram; this is the symbol of the five elements of fire, air, earth, water and spirit or soul. Fives tend to live on their nerves and this can show in excessive worry and upset stomachs. But they have a lot of charm and can keep up a conversation on almost any topic, chatting to anyone about anything. They are naturals at breaking the ice at parties and bringing shyer people out of their shells. They make excellent hostesses and work well in any service industry where they can excel at putting people at ease. Their love of the new brings a passion for the latest gadget and if there is a new computer or phone on the market, they just have to have it!

Number Six – With sixes it is all about harmony. They hate anything disruptive and ugly. Six is linked to the planet Venus and they have a love of beautiful things. Sixes will always have a beautiful home and they make superb interior designers. They also make great artists because they have a good eye for colour and pattern. They love to create art and are often very creative. They tend to love cooking, gardening and fashion; anything where they can exercise their creative skill and spread beauty to the world. They are quite sensual and love food and drink which can lead to weight problems.

Sixes are tactile people who are never afraid to give anyone a hug. If you're upset they'll invite into their beautiful house and feed you and make you tea. Sixes are warm and friendly but they shy from any confrontation and will go to great lengths to avoid arguments; this can make them a bit of a walkover at times because they would rather give in than row. Sixes are also notoriously indecisive for the reason that they hate to hurt people's feeling and so difficult or unpleasant decisions are often deferred. The symbol of six is the six pointed star, also known as The Star of David.

Number Seven – Seven is the number of mysticism. Sevens often live in a daydream, but in their defence they have a strong connection to the Source and tend to live their lives in service to their spiritual needs. Practical concerns interest them less. Seven is ruled by the planet Neptune and so sevens often have a strong affinity with water. Their homes are often close to water and their favourite colours tend to be blue, green or purple. Sevens often excel at photography and cinema because these things are ruled by Neptune.

The symbol of seven is a square with a triangle inside of it; the triangle does not touch the sides of the square. This is symbolic of the soul inside the body; the soul is contained by the body but is a separate entity nevertheless. A lot of sevens will be attracted to alternative religions and they will often be interested in meditation, yoga, chakras and mantras. They will often search for meaning outside orthodox religions. Sevens need to keep their souls happy for no amount of physical or mental stimulation would ever be a substitute for them. It is the nature of a seven to look deeply into life's mysteries. They must always remember that it is not finding an answer that counts but the journey itself. Sevens operate on a higher plane as if they are listening to some sort of celestial music that only they can hear.

Number Eight – Eights are rules by the planets Mars, who was known as The Bringer of War, so they can be aggressive. It is not advisable to stand between an eight and something that they want for they will trample all over you if you get in their way. Eights are not tactful or diplomatic, their way is to charge ahead; life is a battleground to them and they are determined to win. They symbol of eight is two interlocking squares. It is as if the two squares were fighting with each other in a ceaseless battle. Eights do well in scenarios where they can harness their aggression; the military is often where they excel.

Eights do have a lot of energy and are extremely competitive so professional sport often interests them. They have great stamina and rarely get tired. They also enjoy fighting for a cause so legal work or promoting a charity can be beneficial for them. Its important for eights to harness their aggression in positive ways otherwise it will end up getting them into trouble. Eights often have a fiery temper and woe betide anyone who ends up on the receiving end.

Number Nine – Nine is ruled by the planet Pluto which tends to make everyone think of death but it would be more accurate to describe Pluto as the planet of regeneration and this is something that nines excel at. Nines have more energy than all other numbers because it is as if they can bring themselves back to live. They are also extraordinarily good at re-inventing themselves. Nine is the number of endings which can give them a fascination with death making other people think they are quite morbid. The symbol of nine is three interlocking triangles.

Because nine represents of end of things they often like to see how far they can push things or people before they break. Challenging the rules is a very nine preoccupation. Nines are often interested in psychology because they like to get to the bottom of everything. Detective stories will be attractive to them for the same reasons. Nines want to know how it all ends which leads them to the big questions of life and they can be into past lives and life after death experiences. Nines can be attracted to brushes with death involving extreme sports or drugs and alcohol. They need to understand that life is in balance; their symbol of the interlocking triangles represents this. If they push too far, then balance is lost and that can only lead to disaster.

There are two numbers that if your name adds up to them, then you don't break it down further into single figures and that is because these numbers are special power numbers. The numbers in question are eleven and twenty-two.

Number Eleven — Eleven is the number of the teacher. It is interesting that the word 'druid' adds up to eleven because it is quite symbolic of everything that elevens are. Druids were teachers, historians, healers, musicians and poets and all these things are often true of people who are elevens as well. Elevens do not tend to have an easy life at least in the beginning but they tend to be successful much later on in life. The job of an eleven is to instruct other people, sometimes literally and sometimes by example. But elevens are capable of being a very good example or a very bad one; they can be a great influence for good or evil. Elevens see the whole pattern of the world in their own distinctive way and that leads them to what to show others what they see; ultimately they desire harmony but must remember not to force people to the eleven's way against their will.

The best of an eleven is in being an enlightened teacher, who teaches but just subjects, but an understanding and coming to terms with life itself. The worst of an eleven is a dictator who forces everyone to live their way and according to their warped vision. Elevens are always visionaries and are often adapt at realising trends before anyone else does.

Number Twenty-Two – Twenty-two is a very powerful number; these people have a reputation of being either a creator or a destroyer depending on their inclination. One thing that is certain is that they will be hard to ignore. They tend to have a natural sense of charisma that makes them stand out from the crowd. Twenty-twos often have a lot of star quality. Because they are obviously linked to the number four, they are always hard workers but their hard work is more likely to pay off because they have that special sparkle that gets them noticed. Twenty-twos are not usually the sort to work behind the scenes; if they are in a show, it's usually because they are the star.

Twenty-twos can be difficult about sharing the limelight and often have a touch of the diva about them. They know they are the star and they want to make sure that everyone else knows it too. But in their favour, they are extremely good at getting things done, both because they are hard workers and because they are so good at inspiring others. They make great cheerleaders and are great mentors to people who may be younger and more inexperienced than they are.

## Chapter 10: Understanding Numerology

Numerology is the study of numbers and how they affect everything in the universe, including your life. It is an occult science that seeks to uncover the magical and mystical meaning of numbers.

For many years, many scholars and occult practitioners have been fascinated with the study of numbers. It cannot be denied how individuals who share particular traits also share the same life path number, or such numbers that they have learned to embrace in their life.

Just as numbers can give you the measurement of a physical object with precise accuracy, they can also give you certain qualities of anything or anyone that is associated with a particular number.

Just as every star has its place in the sky, it is believed that every man has a number and that this number has a strong influence on his life, and once you master this number, you can master your life.

A brief history

Pythagoras is said to be the father of modern numerology. It is worth noting that numerology has existed far before the time of Pythagoras. Still, Pythagoras must be honored for he had taken numerology to new heights. Instead of focusing on solving mathematical problems as people usually do today, he focused on the meaning and principles behind the math – which was also how the ancients understood and practiced numerology. He realized that just as a triangle can be expressed by giving its proper measurements, the universe can also be expressed through numbers.

Numerology can be traced back in ancient times. It was practiced by the ancient people in Greece, China, Rome, and India, among others. Its origins can be said to be as old as the human race, or even older.

For it is believed that long ago during the time of the ancient gods, numerology was considered a natural language of the universe.

Numerology today

Although numerology still exists and is known worldwide, it is no longer considered normal for the modern man to understand what it really is, much less to know the meaning of every number.

Most people today read numerology for fun. In fact, it is not uncommon to see numerology being placed as part of an entertainment section of a magazine or newspaper, or even in the bookstore. Sadly, the sacredness of its art has been forgotten.

Still, numbers are constant, and the influences that they have on your life have the same power as they have always had centuries ago.

How numbers affect your life

In numerology, it is believed that numbers play a significant role in our lives. Take, for example, your life path number. This number has a continuous effect in your life. In fact, you may notice that undesirable outcomes happen each time you neglect your life path number. Of course, life is more than just following your life path number because all the numbers affect you in ways more than you can imagine. The degree by which each number influences your life varies depending on your present situation.

It is worth noting that in numerology, numbers are not written numbers that you simply add and subtract. Numerology is far different from algebra. In numerology, it is believed that every number has its own unique qualities, traits, and properties. These make numerology go beyond mere mathematics the way most people know it.

The way numbers affect your life depends on the energies that are present around you. In numerology, numbers carry certain types of energies. In fact, numbers themselves are powerful energies. If you can master these numbers, then you can master your life.

Adding numbers

Before you learn about the meaning of every number, it is important to first learn how to add numbers in numerology. The sum of the numbers will be the focal point or the main number that you will "read".

Adding the numbers is very simple. Simply add the digits individually. For example: 4,721 = 4 + 7 +2 +1 = 14 = 5. Hence, the number is 5. Another example: Charles = 3 + 8 + 1 + 18 + 12 + 5 + 19 = 66 = 12 = 3. And another example: October 3, 2006 = 10 + 3 + 2006 = 13 (+8) = 21 = 3.

## Chapter 11: The Beginning

Discover Who You Are

**I AM A** Life Path 5 with an 8 Attitude and a 7 character. If you knew and fully understood numerology, I just gave you the summary of who I am and my background...

Numerology will tell you **who** you are, **how** you will engage in life, and **what** you will become. It will reveal your dreams, character, what you wish for, and how you view the world. Since you do somewhat know yourself, numerology helps validate many things about you and your life. Empowered with knowledge, you can then create a life plan and work with the numbers and cycles to become all that you came into this life to be.

On your life journey, it is essential to surround yourself with like-minded people and distance yourself from those who are not like-minded. How can you move forward if the people who are already experiencing whatever you want to bring into your life are not surrounding you? You can watch, listen and learn to ultimately arrive at your own destination. Don't become disenchanted by what may seem burdens in life; the reality is that you need some life experiences first, to prepare you to move through challenges, in the process, you learn the value of knowing and understanding.

When it comes to relationships, not everyone in your life is a match, nor are they 100% compatible, but there are remedies. When someone drains you of your energy or power, there is a way to change those circumstances. Numerology can show you the challenges so you can implement changes appropriate to your circumstances to master your desired results.

In numerology, four things are revealed from your birth date and three from your birth name. Make note: you can always change your name, but you can never change your birth date. Let's look more closely at those four important elements:

**Life Path:** Reveals the reason you came into this lifetime. This is the road you are traveling and how you will become.

**Birth Day:** Reveals the action steps you take to achieve your Life Path and your character.

**Attitude:** Reveals how you view the world through your eyes.

**Personal Year:** The only number that changes every year to a new cycle, which are cycles 1 through 9.

While the birth date holds four critical elements, there are three important pieces of information that come specifically from your birth name.

**Destiny:** Also called your expression, or personal power. It is calculated by converting all the letters of your birth name to a numerical value—and then continuing to add those numbers until you arrive at a single digit. This reveals what you become, and how you will develop in your professional, social, and personal life.

**Heart's Desire:** This represents your deepest desire…your soul, and your intuition. It is calculated by converting all the vowels to a numerical value—and then adding them to a single digit. This heart's desire is something you share with no one, sometimes not even yourself. Yet this is something you must discover in order to fit all the pieces of your life needed to achieve your desired outcome.

**Personality:** Your personality is how others see you. It is calculated by converting all the consonants in your birth name to a numerical value—then adding those numbers to a single digit. Knowing how to present yourself to others is important to achieve your desired outcome.

In this book you will learn how to calculate these numbers and learn their meaning. I just revealed to you what each means and their importance in your life.

Apply numerology in your life daily and it will change you; in fact it will change the world.

When you listen to your intuition you often receive important messages; however, when you don't pay attention to those messages, the Universe does its best to get your attention in other ways, one of which is through numbers.

Numbers are universal, spiritual, and scientific...in fact if there were no language, we humans would communicate through numbers. We have a calendar, a clock, a birth date, a social security number, a house number, a driver's license number, and of course the Bible is written with numerical references.

There are many numerology books available; this particular one will only benefit you if it resonates with you. With that in mind, I kept it simple. As I am a visual learner, I wrote this the way I learn.

When I first wanted to know and understand the Bible, I read the children's version because it was in story form; it had lots of pictures, which made it easy. I next graduated to a paraphrased bible because it clearly explained the stories by restating the text, which provided another form or meaning I could understand. I was then better equipped to read the American Standard, which is written in today's language; and then—the King James Version.

The point of telling you this is to help you understand that **learning** is a process, and **comprehension** comes in steps. This book can be your first step to understanding the benefits of using numerology in your daily life to change your circumstances and life outcome so you can live your dream life.

After all isn't that what you came here to do? You didn't come here to live a life of lack or pain. If you are experiencing either of these, it's just part of a cycle for you to learn and then... let it go. If you have not been able to do that, then you are not working with the energy of your cycles, and things may just never get on track to your desired results—until you make up your mind to do so.

A word of caution: don't embrace a victim mentally. A wonderful life is yours for the taking if you remain aware and present, and pay attention to the signs and messages given you. Life can be as you choose: a lesson, an experience, or an excuse; a journey, a joy or a joke. Which life are you living right now? What life do you want to live?

Discover Numerology

**NUMEROLOGY IS PART** of the pseudo sciences in the west and yet in the east it is part of everyday practice. Numerology is part of the metaphysical world. Merriam-Webster defines it as:

1. *Relating to things that are thought to exist but that cannot be seen. 2. Relating to the transcendent or to a reality beyond what is perceptible to the senses.
*Source: www.merriamwebster.com

Some things just can't be explained and call for faith-based belief. You can't see air but you know you're breathing it; you are also keenly aware that with no air to breathe you would die. Do we then consider air a pseudo science? You can't sense air, but you know it's there. We actually take breathing for granted.

So it is with personal achievement; a faith-based belief, that once you believe, you can achieve. Having faith in the outcome, the possibilities are endless.

Numerology is another gift that is taken for granted, when in reality, it was given as a tool to live a wonderful life. If you're ready to commit to the process of using this tool because its possibilities resonate with you, then here we go. Enjoy...

Let's look at an enlightening analogy of how you might look at numerology.

In travel you now have the advantages of technology supported by Global Positioning Systems (GPS). What a great analogy... Numerology as a form of GPS, where you can set your destination! You have no idea what route the GPS will map out, but you can trust the GPS will get you to your destination.

Consider this as well: what would happen if you get in the car and don't bother to turn the key? If you just set the destination on the GPS, but don't take action... plain and simple---you're not going anywhere.

The choice is yours... you can choose to be on your way, check in every so often and see your progress; or, alternatively, you can choose to look in the rearview mirror, to see not only where you have been, but how far you have come.

When you come to a roadblock, the sight in the rearview mirror looks familiar, and you find some sense of comfort, believing if you turn around, you know where you've been and what to expect, right? Not!

If you started the journey in the first place because things weren't working, what makes you think going back will be any different? This is the perfect time to resist being reactive and just wait. It is highly possible you are in a down cycle—a time to re-evaluate, rest and plan. When the roadblock clears you will be energized, and excited to move forward again.

Count Chart

**THERE IS a** beautifully mysterious relationship between the letters found in your name, the date of your birth, and how your life is lived out. I share my knowledge of Numerology with you—so you might discover its power—I want to begin your journey where it all starts: the basics of calculating numbers and getting comfortable with tools such as a "Count Chart".

The intention is not to over-simplify the process, because a professionally created Numerology reading will always be more detailed, but to create a comfort zone about the many calculations being addressed, and the tools used to complete them.

How To Begin

The following is a numerology count chart. It is used when letters need to be converted to a number so you can calculate the information.

Everything is calculated to a single digit, unless it is a master number. Master numbers are 11, 22, and 33. A later chapter will focus on master numbers.

| 1 | 2 | 3 | 4 | 5 | 6 | 7 | 8 | 9 |
|---|---|---|---|---|---|---|---|---|
| A | B | C | D | E | F | G | H | I |
| J | K | L | M | N | O | P | Q | R |
| S | T | U | V | W | X | Y | Z | |

How to Calculate

The Birth Name Example: This is where you use the count chart.

Mary Johnson

| M | A | R | Y | J | O | H | N | S | O | N | |
|---|---|---|---|---|---|---|---|---|---|---|---|
| 4 | 1 | 9 | 7 | 1 | 6 | 8 | 5 | 1 | 6 | 5 | 53 |
| This person has an Expression number of (5 + 3) | | | | | | | | | | | 8 |

Birth Name:

The pieces of information you get from the birth name include:

**Your destiny:** your complete birth name converted to a single digit.

**Heart's desire:** the vowels in your birth name converted to a single digit.

**Personality**: the consonants of your birth name converted to a single digit.

Birth Date Example:

The pieces of information you get from the birth date include:

**Life Path:** All the numbers in your birth date.

**Day Number**: The day you were born to a single digit.

**Attitude**: Your month and day added together

**Personal Year**: Your Attitude added to the current year.

The **Life Path:** calculated by adding all the numbers of the birth date:

Example: 10/16/1950

1+0+1+6+1+9+5+0=23
2+3=5

The **Attitude:** calculated by adding the month and day: 1+0+1+6=8

The **Day:** calculated using just the day you were born, if it's a single digit then that's it.

1+6=7

The **Personal Year: is calculated** when you add your attitude number to the current year.

| Attitude | Current Year | Personal Year |
|---|---|---|
| 1+0+1+6=8 | 2+0+1+5=8 | 8+8=16/7 |

Personal Years are calculated from year to year, but you feel the change in the vibration cycle around your birth date.

Depending on your birth date you may feel two vibrations in the same calendar year.

## Chapter 12: What Is Numerology?

The first thing that you must learn is what exactly numerology is. Numerology has a specific set of terms and ideas attached to it, and it's important to know what exactly it is and what it entails for a person if they so choose to get into it. This chapter will help to shed light on this, for it will show you just what in the world the basics of numerology are, and what exactly it is.

Numerology at the bottom of it all is the study of numbers. But it's not just studying the numbers that you see, but you should also look at how it relates to the certain aptitudes and even some traits and tendencies. It's studied in an occult manner, and it relates to a general cosmic plan that they believe the universe has.

Now, how this works is the following. Each letter that is out there has a certain number to it, and it brings about a cosmic vibration that can be derived from it. If you take the full sum of the numbers that are in your birth date, and the sum of the value that you get from the letters in your name, you will then be able to extrapolate a sort of interrelation between this, and you can see the way the vibrations work. These numbers work together to show a great amount of what the character, purpose in life a person has, what motivates them, what their future will be like, and even the talents that they might have hidden within.

There are experts in numerology that use these numbers to help decide what they're going with life, and what is the best time to execute major movies and different activities that you so choose in life.

Numerology can help you with other factors as well, some that you might not invest, when to marry, when to travel, when you should change jobs or ask for a promotion, and even when and where to relocate. This set of studies can help you get a good feel for what you're going to do in life, and with this, you'll be able to take control of your life.

You're probably wondering if this works. Well, the truth is, it is a prediction. The main question you will have is why it works, and how it works. Well, the reason why this sort of thing works might be because of the way the path of life and the cosmos affect us. It does work, but you should always take into consideration the fact that it might not be a perfect system, but it is still a system that you can use in order to help you determine the future and what your life will end up like. It can be something that you will start to learn over time, and you can use this as a guideline to help you determine future actions, and what you should do next. You should still have the decision at the end of the day, because your fate is in your hands, but having this around as a way to help you really get into the different factors of numerology can help you understand, and you can use it in order to better your life.

Usually, this belief is mostly in the divine and the mystical relationship between these numbers and events. It is often associated with the paranormal, along with astrology and even divinity as well. However, there is no scientific evidence for this. You can however start to place faith in these patterns, and you'll able to use this to even help with analyze of various objects and elements in life. If you're looking for signs as to whether or not you can do something, this can be something that can help you.

Now that you know about numerology at the basis, it's time to get some more information, such as the history of it, and you can then see for yourself just what exactly numerology is and what it can do for you.

## Chapter 13: What, Really, Is Numerology?

One thing I can say for sure, even if I was not read — that is, if I were to make an educated guess — is that this long word has something to do with numerals. And those ones I came across when I was learning to count.

But for real, numerology is a kind of analytical tool that uses numbers to help us understand our personality; strengths; talents; challenges; inner needs; emotional predisposition; and so on.

The term comes from the word numeral, and as you, very likely, already know, numerals represent numbers. Of course, someone could poke holes at that definition, because it appears to be equivalent to pure arithmetic, and we will not dwell too much on that because we agree numerology is not pure math. However, what we do underline is that everything within numerology is based on numbers. Even when we bring in the spiritual angle of numerology – as it, definitely, is there – we do, still, use numbers.

Why not be content with feedback from friends and family?

You see, there are those qualities that you display but we are not comfortable asking you to change. There are also other qualities that you do not display, but they still exist in you and they do affect your life, sometimes adversely. But numerology breaks down your character, and since here you have no reason to worry about bias or prejudice, you are ready to accept the reality of whom you are and hence act accordingly.

In essence, numerology helps you to appreciate your different characteristics and how you are predisposed to behave, and you can then use that knowledge to consciously change the way you react to issues and situations; or even the way you handle family, friends, and other people in general.

Just to give a simple example, if you knew that it takes you very little provocation to snap at someone, would you not refrain from making remarks on the spur of the moment when someone tries your patience? Yet without that knowledge, you are likely to see every instant of snapping as an isolated case that you could easily ignore.

So, what obvious benefits accrue from numerology?

You will be amazed at how empowered you will feel with the knowledge and appreciation of numerology. Here are the obvious advantages:

Utilizing opportunities

Once you understand how numerology works, you are at an advantage when it comes to economic and social opportunities that suit your predisposition. It is pretty easy for someone to identify the rice from the chaff and make use of appropriate opportunities in good time. For instance, if two opportunities came up simultaneously, one in the teaching profession and another one in the military, you could easily judge that pursuing a career in the military might be bad for you; that is, when you happen to be – as far as numerology goes – a two.

As you will soon see, two's are known for their friendliness and sweetness; often with the risk of the friendliness dropping to diminishing self-confidence. Surely you cannot go up the ranks in the military when you cannot display boldness and firmness.

Appreciating your talents

When you are well versed with the workings of numerology, you are able to say with confidence what talents you possess – those that you can invest in without having mixed feelings about.

Ability to objectively assess your life

If ever there is a persistent conflict within your family or friends, for example, you can easily tell if aspects of your character are coming in the way of a resolution. If so, you can work on it and hence facilitate mutual agreement.

By the same token, you can use numerology to understand people who are close to you; and if you know the reason they behave the way they do – that is in an unpleasant sense – you will allow yourself to give them more leeway than you otherwise would. That in itself brings harmony in your home and between you and your close friends.

When did people begin to relate numbers with behavior?

Let us say, numerology is thousands of years old; around 10,000 of them. But in its organized form, it is generally accepted that it has got a lot to do with Pythagoras, he of the Pythagoras Theorem and other famous theorems. He is said to have polished the field in Greece around 2,600 years ago. Still, there is this American, L. Dow Balliet, who is credited with having worked with other like-minded people to modify numerology to the way it is today.

In short, numerology has been tried over many years by people of different cultures and faiths; and, gladly, it still holds true. Numerology, therefore, is nothing to be anxious about, but rather, something you would enjoy trying out, even if for fun.

## Chapter 14: Advisor And Teacher/Creator

Jupiter rules the number 3. Jupiter reigns strongly in some part of a chart for anyone born on a 3 day. Jupiter is the only planet whose orbit around the Sun is approximate its numerological value, 11.86 years, which most closely rounds off to 12 years, or the number 3. 3s are eternally youthful. A 3 Birthday is a good example of the extrovert/introvert combination. A 3 enjoys being "out there," but because of it strong individualistic make up, the 3 also craves solitude, especially if the Façade number is a 3. A 3 often is the proverbial "Renaissance Man of many talents." The late Indian metaphysician Harish Johari, born on the 21$^{st}$ exemplified this. Johari has written books on a variety of subjects, including numerology, and also was the guide for Richard Alpert, the American psychologist who later became known as Ram Das. He gained a reputation for bridging Hindu thinking to the West. On the down side, the Renaissance Man can turn into the "jack of all trades, master of none." A couple of strong Pinnacles can help balance this out.

Jupiter's Sanskrit name, "Guru," means teacher. In Roman Mythology, Jupiter was the teacher and leader of the Gods. Teaching and being advisors are areas in which 3s do well because of the ability to think on their feet and their strange combination of youthful thinking and wise old man mindset. 3s can succeed in any sort of career, but for them, most jobs are merely jobs. The only warning for any 3 is do not waste your time or your life. In spite of Jupiter being the teacher, 3s aren't always the most patient people. This especially holds true when the chart holds multiple 3s, or a single 4 or 8 Pinnacle as 4 and 8 are more grounded and rooted numbers and more likely to see a project through to the end, where 3 may become bored and want to move on to something else.. As pure gurus, 3s don't do too badly either, as comes through in the writings of the late Jiddu Krishnamurti of India. When 3s control their mental energy, they also succeed as administrators, supervisors, or political leaders.

The number 3 connotes movement, spirit, and the most extreme fortune at both ends of the spectrum. The resilience and luck of Jupiter came out during the 1994 comet fragment bombardment of the planet. From July 16 through July 22, 1994, more than 20 fragments of Comet P/Shoemaker-Levy 9 collided with the gaseous planet Jupiter. The total force of all the particles was equivalent to that of several large megaton nuclear warheads, yet the fat and sassy Jupiter just kept on spinning through space with only temporary scars in its atmosphere. 3s are great talkers and mixers, but still very individualistic. A 3 Birthday is a good example of the extrovert/introvert combination.

3s, at times, become frustrated because the information they pass along isn't understood for its true meaning. In the movie "2001: A Space Odyssey," the monolith that helps the apes learn to use their forepaws to grasp objects comes from Jupiter, and it is on Jupiter that the fated astronaut is taught the ultimate abstract meaning of life. In the movie "2010," again, it is Jupiter that gives Earth the message to cease war and hostilities, and to share the fruits of space exploration. The monoliths had been set for the right reasons but used for the wrong purpose. Teaching of all sorts is definitely one of the things 3s do well. This teacher side is enhanced by their ability to think on their feet.

3s need to channel and control their physical and mental energies. When 3s control and center their mental energy, they do well as administrators, supervisors, or leaders. Whether they are in the foreground of leadership depends on who they interact with. They also have a problem combining their leadership and abilities with their need for physical freedom and individuality.

Hermann Goering, the commander of the German Luftwaffe and the Minister of Armaments during the Second World War was a good example of this. He had been an Air Force ace in the German Air Force during World War I, but in his duties under Hitler, he was very ineffectual because, as those close to him knew, his mind remained flying among the clouds where he had spent the most memorable time of his adult life. Jiddu Krishnamurti solved this problem of combining physical freedom with a leadership role. He owned nothing other than a few personal items he would carry with him and he lived with friends and followers wherever he taught and lectured.

Many 3s don't experience their greatest success until middle age. This is especially true about people born on the 12th.

Often the palm of a 12 Birthday doesn't show a strong Fate Line until midlife or it breaks off at the Head Line and starts again. This slower growth partly comes from 3s not being materialistic for the sake of materialism. They enjoy using material comforts but can just as easily discard them, which is part of the 3's "guru" nature. In essence, the 3 is the Birthday number most likely to wonder what it will do once it grows up. All he truly needs to do is follow his passion, and the cards will fall into place. It's not unusual for a long string of changes and personal failures to both hinder the progress of 3s and help them find their ultimate, true vocation and "Dharma," the essence of their being.

Abraham Lincoln, a true 12 Birthday suffered from manic-depression and had gone through divorce and bankruptcy by the time he got into politics. However, in true to form manner of the 12/3 resilience, he successfully managed the United States through the most difficult war of its history, the bloody Civil War, and in the history of our planet. The 3 needs to set limits and schedule plenty of playtime for his multitude of brainstorms and mental meandering. Because the physical resilience of Jupiter carries into the 3 Birthday, these natives need to watch for physical excess. Country and western singer George Jones, another 12 Birthday, kept up his heavy drinking and drug abuse until his second Saturn return close to the age of 60.

The 3rd and the 30th probably are the most inherently stable of the 3s. A 12 Birthday can talk himself into or out of almost any situation if he plans far enough ahead. People born on the 21st tend to be the most rigid of the 3 Birthdays. The 3's Moon influence makes them seem softer and less independent than they really are, but dig a bit deeper and you'll come up against the less flexible and more independent Sun- influenced 1. Because of the moon/sun combination, 21 and 12

Birthdays are philosophical neighbors, but from opposite ends of the spectrum.

3s driven by a sense of duty and obligation make the best leaders and administrators. One good example of the positive end of the 3 as an administrator, as well as being quick on his feet, was Benjamin Disraeli, born on the 21$^{st}$, who was Prime Minister under Queen Victoria during England's modern rise as a world power. Abraham Lincoln did not want to run for the Presidency until he fully believed that the United States needed him. 3s have much energy and are at their best when they are motivated by a specific cause or passion. Otherwise, this immense energy easily turns into hours, days, or weeks of obsessing over trivial pursuits or worrying about unnecessary things. The natural actor side of the 3 helps them fit into any sort of work they choose and sometimes into professions they aren't content with. They truly need to be careful what they strive for.

3s can be very experimental in all walks of life, but ultimately, they are traditionalists. Charles Darwin created quite an intellectual and social debate with his theory of evolution, however, he turned down an offer by his contemporary, Karl Marx, to dedicate one of his books, Das Kapital, to Darwin.

Reinhard Gehlen, born on the 3$^{rd}$, began his military service during the Weimer Republic period under the Kaiser. Then he became head of the German Army intelligence units on the Russian front for the Nazis. After the Nazi surrender, he went to work for West German Intelligence and the Central Intelligence Agency during the Cold War. He served all three governments without hesitation because of his traditionalist sense of duty and honor. The only word of caution for them is not to get too close to the dark side, but when they do, it's usually as administrators of nefarious action, as with Hermann Goering, whose wanderings led him into the inner circle of the Nazis, and Charles Manson, who did not participate in the Tate/La Bianca killings but planned and ordered the entire escapade. Galen, while head of West German Intelligence, had a spotless personal record without any known vices, but he used other people's vices to the benefit of the intelligence agency he worked for. Galen never touched the dark side but he skillfully employed others to do so for him repeatedly.

However, nefarious behavior usually comes from an ill placement of Uranus in the astrological chart, and a 12 who winds up on the dark side often is a bungler at whatever he gets himself into. Hermann Goering, the Minister of Armaments in the Third Reich, and Aleister Crowley, the metaphysician who was addicted to heroin until his dying day, are good examples of the 12/3 falling over the edge of the dark side. Their leadership and administrative abilities always need to be channeled in the direction of good.

Under all circumstances, 3s need to keep their creative spark alive through a hobby, even if they don't make their living through the arts. The opposite end of this spectrum is that 3s often make the best gurus, teachers, as the Sanskrit name implies, and as Jupiter was to the rest of the Roman gods. A 3 can easily escape into his own little world and manage to live there without anyone's help, which others sometimes interpret as antisocial behavior. A 1, 3, 4, 7 or 9 Façade number can lessen the appearance of this seemingly anti-social behavior. This very personally created world makes for the most fluidly creative literature, such as the surreal works by the German writer Franz Kafka, born on the 3rd. He lived a financially comfortable life free from political or social persecution. He wrote 'Metamorphosis," about a man who wakes up as a cockroach before the popularization of science–fiction/fantasy. Another of his novels, "The Trial," about a man on trial for no apparent reason, was the basis for the cliché "Kafkaesque.". The only ongoing challenge for the 3 is not to get too caught up in the chase of life for any one thing in particular, but to decide what is most important to him intrinsically. The 3 should enjoy the adventure of the chase, and when, at some point in time, he decides where he wants the chase to take him, steer his life in that direction. 3s also need to be careful not to become up obsessed with time wasting activities that can keep them from their goals.

A 21 Birthday is the most rigid of the 3s, and has the most discipline of all 3s. This particular 3 combination suggests strong and rigid significance, such as the sign of Virgo, in one's astrological chart.

A 3 Façade number is a mixed blessing for the 3 Birthday. It increases the boom/bust cycle of luck. A 2 Façade does little to help a 3 Birthday and a 5 Façade could go far towards helping the playful 3 Birthday get into trouble, but all the remaining façade numbers would help the 3 Birthday keep his independence.

Sexually and romantically by nature, 3 is a more playful number. A 3/1 marriage works best if the 1 is the female. His more dominant personality might sometimes be domineering but the equally independent nature of the 3 female, coupled with her inherent domestic qualities, would strike a balance and would provide for the more traditional family relationship from last century where the male is the more dominant counterpart.

A female 1's independence and aloofness might be too abrasive for the ego of a 3 man, and might not be as driven as his wife. A 1 husband and a 3 wife would be another traditional marriage like that of the 2 female and the 1 man, except that the 3 female would be able to develop interests outside the marriage. A 2/3 marriage works best if the 2 is the female and makes for the traditional marriage. The 3 has more self-discipline for the more difficult times and could be the emotional pillar of the relationship, providing the 2 is willing to open up emotionally. If the 2 is the man, the 3 woman might have too much energy for him and the 3 would have to take the lead.

## Chapter 15: Combining The Core Elements

Some numbers combine more easily than others. It's easiest to think of the numbers in pairs before trying to link them as a full set. You need to think of the base meanings of the numbers in order to work out how they combine. If your numbers don't conflict, your life is likely to be easier and you can be more true to your inner nature. If they conflict, you may struggle with issues and feeling pulled in different directions.

If you have two of the same numbers, this shows that there is an important challenge you need to overcome. Odd numbers tend to combine well with other odd numbers, while even numbers combine well with other even numbers.

1/5, 6/9, and 2/3 fluctuate according to your level of maturity

4/5, 8/11 and 6/7 are almost always discordant

6/2 and 3/6 are almost always in harmony

HABIT CHALLENGE

Your bad habits, what you overdo or don't do enough.

Your habit challenge is made up of the total letters in a name added together. Rather than adding the value of each letter, you add the total number of letters together and reduce them to one single digit.

It is a talent you were born with that may be excessively intensified in your life expression. Stress and confusion often create the reactions found in the habit challenge. Once you become aware of these reactions, you can choose to bring the extremes into balance. Your challenge is to learn how to balance its influence.

1

The issue is of leadership and control. When under balanced, you are indecisive and procrastinate. This leads to feelings of insecurity, dependence and passivity. You

you may be over-attached to your beliefs. You can learn to find original solutions to difficult problems.

The issue is of peacemaking. When under balanced, it's hard to maintain a sense of identity because of a desire to please. It is indecisive, dependent and uncertain. When over balanced it's fussy over small things and caught up in details. You may be oversensitive, disapproving and unsupportive. You can learn to be a good follower and collaborate with others.

The issue is of expression. As an under balanced habit, you can exaggerate, be indulgent and lack direction. You may be unfocused and anxious. When over balanced, it can lead to scattered energies and finding it hard to focus. You can learn to use your imagination and creativity to resolve problems.

The issue is of form. You may expect a lot from others and fail to commit yourself. You are disorganised and uncertain. When under balanced, you are too serious and careful, often creating opposition. You fail to see the details because of getting too caught up in the bigger picture. You risk being antagonistic. You can learn to set reasonable goals, find practical solutions and remain calm.

The issue is of freedom. You respond in an under-balanced way by escaping reality through self indulgence. You are likely to be cautious and doubtful. With an over balanced response you risk changing direction too often before achieving results. You risk being erratic, impulsive and careless. You can learn to take risks and be versatile.

The issue is of responsibility. When it's under balanced you may try to avoid your responsibilities. You risk being distant, self seeking and disorganised. When it's over balanced, you may live through others or offer unsolicited advice. You risk being discontented, overemotional and over-responsible. You can learn to be sympathetic to the needs of others.

The issue is of individuality. You may be over-analytical and critical and become cut off from your own feelings. You risk being superficial and undeveloped. An over-balance makes you detached and hold onto resentments. You risk being resentful, hypercritical and secretive. You can learn to reject unsought advice.

The issue is of manifestation. You may lack material success and motivation. When under balanced it uses work characteristics in home life. You risk being intimidating and manipulative to obtain results. You may try to do everything yourself and be pushy and tactless. You can learn to be efficient and ruthless when resolving difficult problems.

The issue is that of compassion. When under balanced, you may be cold and detached. You are at risk of being passionless, oppressive and aloof. When over balanced, you may be an impractical dreamer and too generous for your own good. You can learn to be broad minded and generous to others.

The master numbers aren't used with habit challenges. They can be read as their reduced vibration.

INTENSIFIED NUMBERS

The number of times a number appears in your name shows its intensity. Repetition of numbers can show special talents while an absence suggests an issue relating to the nature of the number. The average name has 15 to 19 letters. If your name is longer or shorter, you need to adjust your calculations. These calculations are based on English names, and in a non-English name the frequencies of letters will differ.

These energies can help you to gain insight in various ways. You can learn to understand why you repeat certain patterns; point to where you may feel an inner void; point to areas where you may lack experience or development; show you why you rely on certain skills or show where you obsess or have a hidden passion.

The numbers 1, 5 and 9 are found most often in a name and relate to your initiative, freedom and resilience. The numbers 2, 3, and 4 are usually only found once within a name. Sometimes 3 will be repeated, showing a desire for creativity and self-expression.

If numbers that usually only appear once occur more often, they are doubled (or tripled) in force. The number 7 is often missing, so this is not significant. When 7 is present, it shows a desire to prove, reason and understand. The number 8 is also often missing. Successful people often lack an eight.

|  |  |  |
|---|---|---|
| 1 | AJS | 3-4 |

| | | |
|---|---|---|
| 2 | BKT | 1 |
| 3 | CLU | 1 |
| 4 | DMV | 1 |
| 5 | ENW | 3-4 |
| 6 | FOX | 1 |
| 7 | GPY | 0 |
| 8 | HQZ | 0-1 |
| 9 | IR | 3 |

GROWTH NUMBER

Simply look up the numbers of the letters in your first name and add together, reducing if necessary.

Your growth number is based on your first name. Although a significant number, it isn't felt as intensely as your Destiny number. Your first name reveals your day-to day life. However, if you have a nickname that you use, or a shortened version of your name, then this might be more suitable to calculate as a Growth number.

Your first name represents your personal self. It sets you apart from other members of your family, whereas your last name represents your family traits and inherited qualities.

The first letter and first vowel found in your first name are also important. These two letters describe your reactions and responses. The first letter offers clues to how you respond to the outer world. The first vowel provides insight into how you respond to your dreams and motivations. When the first letter is also a vowel, you use the first letter to represent both concepts.

You will grow through asserting your individuality.

You will grow through relationships with others.

You will grow through the way you use your words and creativity.

You will grow through dealing with your fears and making yourself secure.

You will grow through learning to use your freedom.

You will grow through having love in your life.

You will grow through gaining spiritual wisdom.

You will grow through learning to manage money and power.

You will grow through using compassion and forgiving those who hurt you.

You will grow through learning spiritual truth.

You will grow through learning to trust your intuition.

You will grow through sacrificing yourself when necessary, without becoming a martyr.

## Chapter 16: Your Astrology

As we have seen, there is a lot to consider when it comes to learning your personal astrology. There is a lifetime's worth of studying that could be done to analyze the heavens and how they affect you and your surroundings. Many people memorize their sun sign and leave it at that; this is only scratching the surface of your specific astrology. While memorizing all the planets at once is a daunting task, it is recommended that starting with the sun, moon, and ascendant be studied first since they have some of the most influential qualities of the natal chart.

Learning this esoteric art is a lifelong task, but there are many simple ways to implement astrology into your life. Timing certain events, predicting the future and working with the specific planets and signs to improve yourself are only a few practices in the expanse of the heavens. While there is no reason for us to go into why or how it works, there are many theories. Some believe that the planets and stars have an actual physical effect on the earth and its inhabitants. Some believe that some actual gods or spirits reside on or in these planets in dimensions humans cannot see. Others believe that the heavens simply offer insight into ourselves and acts as a symbolic mirror of events on earth. Perhaps it is simply a very efficient calendar. Maybe it is all these things. Regardless of what you choose to believe about the true nature of reality, astrology will help you in some way. Whether it's communicating with spirits or just psychological analysis, the heavens are powerful and if you pay attention to them, they will pay attention to you.

In today's society, we can simply use technology to help us keep track of our personal chart and any transits. It is highly recommended that you download an astrology app that calculates your natal chart and offers some insight into its aspects. There are many, many apps so try a few and pick one that suits you. These apps often have notifications that will keep track of any powerful transits or world events, such as a full moon or disruptive Uranus transiting your natal Mars.

Below we will discuss certain techniques and practices that are common when working with the planets and stars. These techniques are as old as time itself, but we will filter them through a contemporary lens. Use these techniques wisely and be humble when approaching these energies, there are plenty of shared experiences, old and new, that may be adverse effects of using astrology for evil purposes. Be morally upstanding and appreciative of the gifts that the heavens offer.

Your signs

As we mentioned, your sun sign, moon sign and ascendant are the best starting points to begin your journey into astrology. Let's take a look at these influences with more in-depth detail.

Sun Sign

You may know your sun sign already. The sun sign is the sign the sun was placed in at the exact time of your birth. This is what most astrology sites use to write up horoscopes and other personality traits. While the sun sign is probably one of the most important signs, we need to consider all the other planets as well, but this requires a computer program or intense math to calculate. Since our current society relies on a sun-based calendar, we can know what our sun sign is using our well-known twelve-month calendar. The sun signs are as follows:

Aries: March 21 – April 19

Taurus: April 20 – May 20

Gemini: May 21 – June 20

Cancer: June 21 – July 22

Leo: July 23 - August 22)

Virgo: August 23 - September 22

Libra: September 23 - October 22

Scorpio: October 23 - November 21

Sagittarius: November 22 - December 21

Capricorn: December 22 - January 19

Aquarius: January 20 - February 18

Pisces: February 19 - March 20

Find your birthdate and keep a note of your sun sign. Go back to the zodiac and planets section of this book and read up on the qualities of this sign and the sun. Do you see parallels in your life? Are these readings somewhat accurate? Don't be discouraged if it's not describing you in detail; there are many other astrological factors as well that influence your natural makeup.

Take note of the positive and negative effects of certain planets; sometimes you may find yourself being grumpy or unnecessarily upset. Before you are quick to blame yourself, check your natal chart.

Perhaps there's an emotional transit in Cancer or a fiery Mars transit. This is one technique that helps balance your emotional state, instead of getting down on yourself you will see that there are some rough waters ahead in your chart, you will be able to prepare for these times, maybe plan some relaxation time, or give offerings to the troubling planet as a means to soften the blow.

Moon Sign

The moon sign is more complicated to calculate since our calendar doesn't sync up with its cycles as well. We can check our moon sign online or with an app. Once you find your moon sign, check the zodiac and planets section to cross reference the personality traits. The moon moves quite quickly through the zodiac so the more will transit your natal moon about once per solar month. This conjunct aspect will create harmonious moon energy for a couple of days. The phase of the moon will affect this as well, this is easily known by looking up at the night sky, but can also be found out with an app or internet search.

The moon is so fluid that her personality and influence is constantly changing. It is no secret that a full moon night is always a strange one. Depending on what sign the full moon is in, these nights are great for moon workings. Festive socializing and indulgence are common on full moon nights, so if you are trying to plan a party and want to choose a favorable date, choose the next full moon, see what sign it will be in and plan accordingly. Leave an offering for the moon that evening and ask for her good grace.

Aspects

An astrological aspect is a number of degrees that a planet may be from another planet; this creates an angle that has a certain effect on the planet's relationship to each other. These angles can be between two planets or even a planet and the ascendant. These aspects are either considered hard aspects or soft aspects, the hard aspects being more intensive respectfully.

These aspects happen throughout the planetary movement, although some days may not have any notable aspects at all, this is considered relatively calm skies. Planets can be aspect to each other in real time or even create an aspect to your natal planets; for example, Venus could create an aspect to your natal Venus. Aspects also have a specific house they are linked to. Your natal chart will also more than likely have aspects between planets, so it is good to familiarize yourself with how these aspects alter the planet's personalities. Let's explore the hard aspects and their influences.

**Conjunction**

When planets are conjunct, they are very close to each other in the chart, usually within ten degrees of each other. This aspect is thought to be one of the most powerful aspects any two planets can create. Conjunct planets typically have a harmonious quality as the planets work together to create a distinct influence. Depending on the sign that they are conjunct in the planets could work together to because you trouble as well, this is also dependent on your natal chart as well. It needs to be said that sometimes more than two planets can be conjunct to each other. Three or even four planets could be within a few degrees of each other; this can be very complex and intense energy. If three or more planets are conjunct in a natal chart, it is called a stellium. Conjunct aspects are closely linked to the 1st house

**Sextile**

When planets are sixty degrees apart, it is called a sextile aspect. This aspect is considered to be creative and dynamic, often dealing with groups or teamwork. Ease of communication between the planets involved and overall favorable unless poorly represented in your natal chart. This aspect is closely linked to the 3rd and 11th houses.

**Square**

When planets are ninety degrees apart, they are considered a square aspect. It is thought that if an outer planet, Jupiter, Saturn, Uranus, Neptune or Pluto is square an inner planet then the outer planet is usually affecting the inner planet more intensely. This aspect often lends itself to troubling or complicated decision making. This could cause conflict or dramatic crisis. This aspect is closely linked to the 4th and 10th houses.

**Trine**

When planets are one-hundred-twenty degrees from each other, they are considered to be trine. We see the power of three come into play with this aspect; it is considered to be harmonious and progressive, often awakening inner desires or talents that have been dormant. Peace of mind and calming of the storms is brought with this aspect. Conflicts are resolved and expression comes easily. This aspect is closely linked to the 5$^{th}$ and 9$^{th}$ houses.

**Opposition**

When planets are one hundred and eighty degrees from each other, or directly across from each other in a chart, they are considered to be in opposition. Unlike the unification effects of conjunction, opposition aspects create polarity and tension. This can be conflicting, creating a battle between internal and external forces. This isn't necessarily always negative, sometimes opposites attract for a distinct reason, commonly to teach a lesson through intense experience or trying times. This aspect is closely related to the 7$^{th}$ house.

Minor aspects

We have explored the major aspects, but there are minor aspects as well. Many astrologers agree that these aspects are miniscule and have a very subtle effect that may not be worth too much time and attention. Some minor aspects are as follows:

Semi-Sextile – Thirty-degree angle

Quintile – Seventy-two-degree angle

Septile – fifty- one-degree angle

Semi-square – Forty-five-degree angle

We see with these aspects that astrology can get very complex, one may say almost as complex as human personalities. This realization solidifies the fact that sun sign horoscopes and readings alone are not in depth enough to really get any insight into someone's complicated personality. This is why we suggest focusing on the three major astrological planets, sun, moon and ascendant when you are beginning in astrology.

Planetary Hours

Similar to how each day has a planetary ruler, Sunday/Sun, each hour of the day is ruled by a certain planet as well. The order of planets is the same each day but will start with a different planet depending on what day it is. This further details a planet's influence throughout the day, so if a planet is ruling a certain hour, then that planet is that much more influential during that hour. This system uses only the seven classical planets, so Uranus, Neptune and Pluto are left out. The order of planets is known as the Chaldean Order; this comes from ancient Babylonian astrology. The order was developed by taking how long each planet takes to travel the entire zodiac, the slowest to quickest planets as they appear from the earth's perspective. We see an order of planets with our naming of the weekdays Sunday through Saturday, but for planetary hours we will skip three planets backward in this list to know the next hour's ruler. For example, Tuesday is ruled by Mars, so around daybreak, the hour of Mars begins. The next hour will be the hour of the sun since we skip three planets previous of the weekday order:

Sunday – Sun         3

Monday – Moon        2

Tuesday – Mars       1

Wednesday - Mercury

Thursday - Jupiter

Friday – Venus

Saturday – Saturn

And so the order of planetary hours for Tuesday will go:

Mars

Sun

Venus

Mercury

Moon

Saturn

Jupiter

This pattern is the same every day only starting with the ruler of that day. This syncs up with our current order of the weekdays so that every twenty-fifth hour is the following day's planetary ruler and thus a new cycle.

The planetary hours are great for timing certain things. If you are looking to work with the moon, choosing a Monday in the hour of the moon to leave offerings or initiate an activity that is governed by the moon, such as taking a bath, is the most potent. This is why we see a lot of planetary rituals and prayers performed at daybreak or dusk; this hour of the day is usually ruled by that day's planetary ruler.

**Practice**

So how can you apply what you've learned to better yourself and your life? There are many ways to go about this, ancient and more contemporary. Also, keep in mind that you create your own practice as well, there is nothing wrong with an individual routine or technique that you created. If it works, then it works. Let's explore some common uses for astrology in the real world for self-development and personal empowerment.

**Timing**

Sometimes it can be tough to decide when to start a new project, or plan that dinner date. Many people probably do not pay any mind to the fact that if you plan something on an astrologically unfavorable day that it may not go well. Using your natal chart and current chart will help with this.

For example, if you were wanting to get married, it is recommended to so on a favorable day. Don't pick a day when Mars is excited and going to cause conflict and troubles. If you can plan it on a day when Venus is in the 7$^{th}$ house, on the day of Venus, in the hour of Venus then you have a powerful combination for love and marriage, also leaving offerings for Venus will help gain good grace from the beauteous planet.

Take time to plan all major events in this way; it may take more time to plan but imagine how much time you lose when things don't go according to your expectations! Be sure to look at the current configurations of planets. Many apps allow you to cycle ahead and see what the configurations will be on any given day. Pick a time when a favorable planet is in the most suitable house and doesn't have any negative aspects. It also encouraged to keep retrogrades in mind, for instance starting new projects or long journeys is not recommended during Mercury in retrograde.

**Offerings**

Although some people that practice astrology don't adhere to this practice, many ancient systems felt that there were gods or spirits that act as mediators between humans and the heavens. Our ancestors would leave offerings and say prayers for the planets to appease them and avid troubling aspects. This practice is great for the spiritual side of astrology and at the very least helps you build a relationship with the planets.

Setting up a planetary altar to leave offerings at is very useful, although you may leave the offerings outdoors as well. For example, let's use the planet Jupiter. On Jupiter's day, in the hour of Jupiter, light a candle that is white or a color associated with Jupiter, such as a royal purple. While the candle is lit, you can meditate in Jupiter and his personality, maybe say a prayer or ask his good grace. Suitable offerings for any planet include incense, coins, water or herbs. For Jupiter money is ideal, especially if you are seeking material gains from this Jupiter working. Finish up your quiet moment with Jupiter and give thanks. Leave the candlelit if you'd like, or blow it out for future use.

With this practice, it is highly suggested that you study astrological magick to make sure you want to take this route. This type of work is very transformative and should be handled with great care and humility. Be respectful and keep in mind this is not a game; once you start this journey you have the planet's attention, do not ignore them.

World Events

To fill time in between your personal work many astrologers analyze world events. You can pick a major event and calculate its astrology and see how it syncs up with the planetary configuration. This helps you understand the planets and zodiac from a broader perspective. Many choose to calculate the president's natal charts or major shifts in civilization. This can be done for past events or to forecast future events, which we will explore deeper in subsequent chapters.

## Chapter 17: The Power Of The Birthday

Since the immemorial time, people could feel the mysterious influence of numbers. Always the one who could unravel the mystery of numbers, was able to solve the mystery of universal harmony and, perhaps, the mystery of life itself. Even Pythagoras asserted that "everything is a number". He believed that numbers are living some special, independent lives, that they have their own destiny, characters, habits and preferences. And the immemorial time the ancient science of numerology was trying to understand the magic and the inner mystery of numbers.

Numbers are always around us since our birth till the very last moments of our lives. Deliberately or not - we obey their laws. Any word can be reduced to a number, any concept and any character.

The number of birthdays can not be changed, it is constant in human life and it is representing the vibrating effect which is present from the time of one's birth. However, what is the extent to which it can determine a person's character or control his destiny, his future, how it depends on the other factors of numerology?

In theory, two people with one and the same number of birthday should be similar to each other in many respects, but actually it happens very rarely. Most likely, the number of birthdays is just revealing the inherited traits of a given person, his ability to control circumstances; this number is more like a governing factor rather than dominant.

Yet the number of birth has been of paramount importance, as they are guiding people not to act against their natural inclinations. The birthday number is able to help us to see the areas of power that are enclosed in the power of our numerological combinations.

Detailed Readings:

**1st** You are a determined leader in the truest sense and can gain the support and trust of others easily, even when your highly independent self would rather work alone.

**2nd** You are very sensitive and diplomatic, and your warm demeanour is a strength when dealing with or mediating others. Your intuition is strong, tapping you into the inner thoughts of those around you.

**3rd** Whether you've worked at it or not, you have a highly-developed creative talent and are a natural-born artist. Your affectionate demeanour and wit make you a social star.

**4th** You're every employer's dream: a hard-working, detail-oriented individual with high principles. And still, you maintain a sense of compassion for others and a love of close family.

**5th** You're lusty... wanderlust, that is. Your eccentric self loves a change of scene and craves travel and adventure. You are highly adaptable and communicative and relate well to others.

**6th** You're a generous family person, a kind soul with a strong skill in keeping the peace. You are able to resolve the unrest between loved ones by easily finding the best middle ground.

**7th** Your mind is your greatest asset. You enjoy contemplating on any topic, from the scientific to the spiritual and have a great sense of focus. You take nothing at face value and can rely on your strong intuition to find truths that are hidden to others.

**8th** You're an "ideas person" when it comes to dreaming up new ventures, and you back this with a creative approach to business and money matters. You are efficient, realistic and confident in your skills, always up for a challenge.

**9th** Your open mind, relentless optimism and compassion for your fellow man make you true humanitarian. You are charming and well-liked by others, and find it easy to relate to others, regardless of their differences.

**10th** You are highly ambitious and (no surprise!) yearn for independence so that you can follow your dreams however you see fit. Your drive for success is strong, and you can rely on your analytical mind and solid managerial skills.

**11th** You're an optimist, but not naive: your rose-coloured view of the world is matched with a strong sense of confidence and determination. You are a dreamer, and your intuition is highly refined, helping you to reach an understanding of others.

**12th** You are a true artist, bringing creativity to everything from your home and style to the way you express yourself. Your enthusiastic nature, imagination and wit make you the light of your social circle.

**13th** You're "the rock" in your family and community, and dependable above all else. You are organized and detail-oriented, using these skills in everything from nose-to-the-grindstone work to artistic endeavours.

**14th** Globetrotter! Your restless nature flocks toward the unexpected twists and turns of travel and variety. While you possess an analytical mind, on the outside you are a very social, communicative and lucky person.

**15th** Your creative spirit pushes you toward artistic expression. While you possess strong instincts in business and financial matters, your sensitivity and range of talents makes you accessible to those around you.

**16th** Never quite at home in the "real world," you love to concentrate your focus on big ideas. Your interests lie in the spiritual and philosophical realms of life, and your intuition is excellent.

**17th** Your lofty ambitions and towering goals are balanced out by your grounding skills in finances and business. Your judgment is practical and efficient and your confidence level is high, motivating you to meet the expectations of others, and yourself.

**18th** Not only are you a natural leader, but your leadership also inspires others. You have a keen understanding of other people, and could be an efficient manager or politician. You are broad minded and able to express yourself well.

**19th** You are highly ambitious and thrive on independence. Your pioneering, risk-taking nature is balanced with creativity and sensitivity to help you succeed in a wide variety of endeavours.

**20th** You're like a mood ring, reflecting the emotions, desires and fears of the people who surround you. Your intuition and sensitivity are strong, and you must fight to keep a healthy distance from others.

**21st** Your creative visions and unique ideas are propelled by your determination to succeed. Your imagination is the driving force behind nearly everything you do, and your passionate nature is reflected in your love of other people.

**22nd** You have a strong professional drive and flock toward innovative business rather than supporting the status quo. Your greatest strength is in your unusually dualistic perception: you are able to envision what you want and actually make your desires materialize.

**23rd** You love change, excitement and risk, and thankfully, you are quite adaptable and easy to get along with. Your skills in affection and communication are strong, and your creative, versatile mind loves the experience of something new.

**24th** You are family-oriented, with a gift for restoring and maintaining balance, peace and harmony in relationships. You are an emotional soul who is willing to sacrifice for the good of others. Your strongest skills lie in healing and meditation.

**25th** Your rational, analytical mind is balanced with strong intuition, giving you the gift of broad knowledge and understanding to help you make the best decisions.

**26th** Your strong sense of business and financial affairs is supported by a creative, daring mindset, making you a confident and capable professional leader -- just don't lose sight of the details within the bigger picture.

**27th** You make an efficient manager, capable of organizing the facts and inspiring others. Your knack for creativity and expression, paired with a strong understanding of others, helps you excel in such diverse fields as politics, art and law.

**28th** You have a gentle air of authority about you, but feel more comfortable leading others when there's a sense of cooperation and teamwork. While your mind is rational, your thinking is unconventional and idealistic.

**29th** You have a rich imagination and a visual approach to every area of your life. Your intuition is your greatest asset, and your connection to higher spiritual forces is strong.

**30th** You are an artist to your very core. You are a sociable person, and others perceive you as a charming and inspiring individual. While you seek harmony in all that you do, you must always remind yourself to balance your imagination with a sense of discipline.

**31st** Your love of family and tradition make you a solid foundation amongst loved ones. You draw appreciation and support from co-workers because of your affinity toward order, discipline and details. You are urged to make the most of the many opportunities you will encounter.

The month of Birth in Numerology

Birth month, or month of birth in numerology, gives an indication of how our younger, more formative years will influence our adult lives.

– January

If you were born in January, the number 1 will be a focal point in your early years. You have somewhat of an independent nature and tend to form your own ideas regardless of other's views. You spend a great deal of time by yourself and therefore have the ability to reflect with an analytical style of introspection. You are a born leader and set the pace that others follow. You can, however, have a propensity for making decisions which affect others without first consulting them, so you may need to take others into consideration in order to maintain harmony. You have a creative flair and enjoy working in an environment where you have autonomy and can make an impact on your milieu.

– February

If you were born in February, the number 2 will be important to you as you are able to use your intuition to help you through those times when you feel unsure. Women will play a significant role during your early years as they help determine what type of education you will receive, ultimately playing a part in the vocation you will opt for as an adult. Personal relationships will be important to you as you develop close alliances that will be cultivated throughout the years. You are quite sensitive and can be hurt easily by tactless words said in haste.

– March

If you were born during March, the number 3 will figure prominently in your life. You are considered lucky because quite often you will find yourself exactly at the right place at the right time to take advantage of a once in a lifetime opportunity. You are able to manage your money well and therefore have a significantly higher standard of living than others who are on similar budgets. As a general rule, you possess a sunny disposition which attracts friends and acquaintances, thus forming an active social life. You can, however, suffer bouts of depression, which may require professional help to ensure that these dark moods do not progress into something more serious.

– April

If you were born during April, the number 4 will have a strong influence in your early years as you work to develop self-control as a mechanism to achieve what you desire. You possess a personal magnetism which will draw people to you, so you, therefore, should not find yourself alone as you have a large circle of friends and acquaintances to keep your diary full. While you are a born leader who can take charge of any situation, there will be occasions when you need to ask yourself whether you are taking control for the greater good of all or your own personal interests. When distressed, you may have a tendency to direct anger at yourself rather than risk offending others, which could cause you to become depressed, overindulge or develop psychosomatic illnesses.

– May

If you were born in May, the number 5 will play a significant role in your life. You tend to be very communicative and even if not prone to talkativeness, you will nonetheless express this trait by extensive reading or writing. You have high respect for authority which makes you a generally dependable person. You believe in the sanctity of marriage and therefore prefer to have any serious relationship formalized with a ceremony to cement the bond. You prefer to spend your free time in the pursuit of pleasure and enjoy socializing with friends and family.

– June

If you were born in June, the number 6 is significant as you can be pleasant and attract a variety of people to you. Although you yearn for that soulmate connection that poets have described throughout the ages in poetry and prose, true unity often seems to elude you because quite often another person will be involved to complicate any liaison. While you may not personally have reservations about letting your attention wander, you can become jealous of anyone who you perceive to be competition, additionally, while you can be the soul of discretion, you are not above spreading rumours if you feel that it will further your career or make life difficult for your adversaries.

– July

If you were born in July, the number 7 will be significant to the building of your character. You are genuinely sincere and this trait attracts people to you because they feel listened to. Because you possess a will of iron, you are able to use your drive to achieve goals. Home is paramount, and you will go to great lengths to ensure the family unit remains intact. While you are generally considerate of others, you can react with more than a bit of cattiness when you feel under the weather.

– August

If you were born in august, you will strongly identify with the number 8. You are a responsible individual who can be counted on to carry projects through to completion and for this reason, you can be relied upon to organize get together and outings. You are a loving person and tend to crave satisfying friendships, romance, children and animals to share your life. Because you are able to maintain an enduring disposition even when circumstances are less than ideal, you have the propensity to develop stress-related health problems as psychosomatic responses which you try to keep under control.

— September

If you were born in September, the number 9 will be highly significant in formulating your character. You may find that your lifestyle will change quite suddenly and without notice, so it would, therefore, be wise to save for a rainy day to help you through those lean times which will periodically come. You need to stay busy, either by necessity or choice and will find responsibilities help the day to go by much faster. While you are a highly intelligent person, you will go to great lengths to conceal your true aptitude because an innate sense of modesty considers such displays to be inappropriate.

– October

If you were born in October, the number 10, which is a higher vibration of 1, will be highly placed in your life. You are considered to be lucky because you have a knack for being at the right place at the right time, thus enabling you to take advantage of the moment. You can be quite focused when you decide upon a certain course of action, and may even find yourself in the midst of occasional power struggles when you encounter another whose goals are at cross purposes to your own. While you possess a pleasant disposition which attracts others to you, there is a dark side to your personality which you reveal only to your closest friends.

– November

If you were born in November, the number 11 which is a higher vibration of 2, will be of great importance to you. You are highly intuitive and if not aware of your sensitivity, may be susceptible to picking up the emotions of others. You place a great deal of emphasis on family ties and feel a responsibility to siblings and parents less fortunate than yourself, even if it causes discord in your own personal relationships. While you possess a sunny disposition, you can suffer from deep bouts of depression, which you will go to great lengths to hide.

– December

If you were born in December, you have a strong affinity to the number 12 which is a higher vibration of 3. You possess an innate philosophical outlook which helps you maintain a stable lifestyle even under the most trying of circumstances. You are unusually lucky with money and will find that you profit through work, investments or inheritances. You have a wide circle of acquaintances which enable you to have an active social life if that is what you desire. You are quite ambitious and will climb the corporate ladder in whatever profession you pursue. While you are understanding and give sound advice, you can suffer from bouts of melancholy which may give you a rather cynical outlook on life.

## Chapter 18: How To Explain Numerology

Do you think it would be reasonable to say that numerology has something to do with numerals? Well, though at this point that assertion may just be a matter of conjecture, you must, of course, have learnt in life the art of putting two and two together – and that can, obviously, be nothing else but four. Numerals, goes without saying, are representations of numbers in whatever form. So, whatever you are going to find in this book about numerology has a lot to do with numbers. Numerology – numerals – numbers... Sounds logical...

Anyway, beginning the serious, but easy to understand, business of numerology, it is that area of study that gets you to see what numbers have to say about your behavior and your attitudes. You get to learn why you seem stuck when you pursue this career but move smoothly when you pursue that other type of career. You get to see why you get along with certain people and not with others. The thing is, you as a human being, have vibrations — energy vibrations. And numbers? Well, they too produce those. And so there is that linkage between your energy vibrations and those that the number relating to you produces to form some form of characteristic. And once you know what number is instrumental to your life success, it is easy to analyze and understand your personality, and also to adapt to varying circumstances.

One thing that may give you comfort is the knowledge that this discipline of numerology has been in operation for many years. The guy credited with initiating it, somehow indirectly, Pythagoras, began working with it almost three centuries ago. Then along came L. Dow Balliett who lived in the 19th century and he made use of his spiritual background with the principles of Pythagoras to bring out the workings of present day numerology. Of course, the discipline has been modified over time, with Balliett's student, Dr. Juno Jordan adding his own input to the discipline in 1972.

Is it fine to memorize number meanings in numerology?

Well, look – in numerology, you just do not deal with abstract numbers. In fact, you need to look at those numbers like they have life. Whether you memorize the meanings or not, the important thing is to understand that whatever number happens to be significant in your life, it has elaborate but clear explanations attached to it. And it is those explanations that you need to analyze in relation to your personal life. For instance, you and I could share the same personal number, but how you use the meaning in that number to improve your life may be different from how I use it. Confusing? Definitely, not… All we are saying is that you need to use your number meanings in context.

Sometimes the numbers that help explain certain aspects of your life best are those derived from astrology. You will even get to learn that your zodiac sign has some information of a personal nature touching on your behavior, aspirations and prospects. And as we have already mentioned, there is life in those numbers – they are not just some inanimate prints when it comes to numerology.

Some Key Benefits attributed to Numerology

If you find a trend that is becoming popular by the day, it may be worth checking it out. There could be something good for you too. And that today is what numerology has become – a specialty that people are seeking to understand, especially because it tells you much about your current life; helps you understand the past you could hardly explain; and shed light into your future.

And you know the beauty of it? Anyone can actually learn numerology thoroughly within a short time and get to practice it almost with precision. Besides that, you do not have to worry about any of your religious folk associating you with magic or witchcraft. This discipline of numerology is all mathematics, thanks to Pythagoras, the great mathematician of days gone by. You do some simple math arithmetic that helps you get a simple number, which then guides you into exploring your potential.

Here are some of the benefits attributed to numerology

Understanding yourself better

It helps you get a relatively good idea how you behave in relation to other people; your likes and dislikes; your fears as well as obsessions; and many of your other tendencies – and all without fear or prejudice.

You can practice numerology without professional help

You do not need to pay someone to decipher the meaning of numbers that are significant in your life. Numerology is something you can learn and understand with ease. In fact, even when numerology is based on numbers and you get to hear of terms like the divine triangle or birth numbers, none of these is anything like the complex square roots of decimals; statistical probability; or such other stuff that can make you call in sick just to duck the math lesson. Calculations in numerology are simple. As a matter of fact, you will get consolation to know that numerology remains within the math of single digits. How simple!

Enhancing your relationships

Numerology can help you solidify your relationships by letting you see what negative aspects of your behavior rub people close to you the wrong way; and also letting you identify what it is you need to demand in your relationship with other people.

Opens your eyes to opportunities

Why waste your precious years training for a career you are naturally ill suited for? From numerology, you will get to see how numbers can give you insight into your traits, letting you see what careers you can fit in and which ones you are better off giving a wide berth.

Numerals are versatile

Did you know you could use numbers to know more than your behavior? Well, that is true. One such example is in using numbers to help you determine if you should settle in a given place or not. In short, the simple arithmetic you do with the address of the place brings out information that points to the suitability or lack of it of living in the particular environment. Of course such information has a lot to do with the energies of the people dwelling in the area vis-à-vis your own energy; the nature of the family units – whether single or couples – and so on.

## Chapter 19: If You Born On The 9. (Ninth) Or 18th (Eighteenth), Or 27th (Twenty Seven) Of Any Month Than Kindly Read The Following:

THE NUMBER NINES

In general, nine are broad minded, idealistic, generous loving people with multiple talents. They are interested in universal good and often go into fields where there is broad scope. Music, Art, drama, healing arts, the ministry, metaphysics, social reform any area is open to them. They have a strong need to express the self, but not necessarily in the more ego-centered way of the One or Eight. Nines can be diffused and vague.

They are very vulnerable to outside influences and often experience difficulty in deciding what they are going to be or in making decision in general. Young Nines may choose an eccentric life style to rebel against tradition.

They may or may not continue on that path depending on who they meet and the experiences that influence them. Nines need to learn not to take everything personally. They will take up causes and wonder why others are not so involved as they are. They will do well in groups that strives to reform and educate. All nines have dramatic style whether in their dress, speech, manner, or philosophy. They can be distant and cool. You can succeed in any artistic, healing, teaching, philanthropic, or musical line of work. You are idealistic and emotional.

Life is serious for you and you feel such a need to be of service to the world that you have trouble making up your mind about which carrier you follow. You are very capable but have some trouble concentrating on everyday details.

You become absorbed in whatever interest you and you have many interests. You may have a metaphysical outlook towards world problems. You will find yourself involved with much group work throughout your middle years. You may travel extensively and your life will always be full of surprises. You may be drawn to transformational work through therapy.

When you multiply any number by 9, then add the resulting digits and reduce them to a single digit, it always becomes a 9. For example, 5 x 9 = 45, reduce 45 to a single digit by adding them together: 4+ 5 = 9. Similarly, 7 x 9 = 63, and 6 + 3 = 9. Or 25 x 9 = 225, 2 + 2 + 5 = 9, and so forth.

When you multiply any number by 9, then add the resulting digits and reduce them to a single digit, it always becomes a 9. For example, 5 x 9 = 45, reduce 45 to a single digit by adding them together: 4+ 5 = 9. Similarly, 7 x 9 = 63, and 6 + 3 = 9. Or 25 x 9 = 225, 2 + 2 + 5 = 9, and so forth. There is nothing similar about this. Any number, no matter how large, multiplied by 9 reduces to 9. From a numerological perspective, the 9 simply takes over, like the infamous body snatchers. Any number that was initially increased by a factor of 9

The more you can be of service to humanity, the greater will be your personal reward on all levels You must have a keen sense of what will work, but at the same time directing those efforts toward some greater good. Your challenge is to find a place for yourself that has some direct benefit to others. Natives born on the 9th day usually take enough time before choosing a clear job or profession.

## Conclusion

You deserve a big pat on the back if you've made it to the end of this book! All done, all finished! Numerology, of reality, is not for everyone. Many may consider all the figures daunting and confusing, while others actually "get it" and thrive on the difficulty of sorting it out. When you are one of the lucky people who "get it," then start planning for a big transition as your life is not going to be the same.

Now that you can better know yourself and others, and now that you have your life's roadmap, you're one move ahead of the game—that's the game of life! You have risen to a life of prosperity in which you can draw on your experience and play a better game with an appreciation of your numbers. The gift of insight is priceless, and you have it in the palm of your hands thanks to numerology!

For work or pleasure, you can use numerology and calculate the charts for your colleagues, loved ones, and friends. Just be diplomatic and compassionate when communicating sensitive information such as lessons in life, weaknesses, and challenges. Being an effective and competent numerologist requires dedication, persistence, and effort, and being careful with this expertise when you reach that level. Some people will believe all you say, so be gentle in your approach and let them know that you are still learning.

www.ingramcontent.com/pod-product-compliance
Lightning Source LLC
Chambersburg PA
CBHW072014070526
44583CB00015B/1473